W0328978

Accelerate

A SKILLS-BASED SHORT COURSE

LOWER INTERMEDIATE 2

Series editor: Philip Prowse

SUE BAILEY • SARA HUMPHREYS

HEINEMANN ELT

Heinemann English Language Teaching, Oxford

A division of Macmillan Publishers Limited

Companies and representatives throughout the world

ISBN 0 333 74196 X

First published 1995

Designed by Ken Vail Graphic Design
Cover design by Threefold Design
Cover photograph by Frank Orel/Tony Stone Images
Illustrated by: Mike Badrocke, Ilsa Capper, Debbie Clark, Jo Dennis, Nick Hawken, Mike Lacey, Gillian Martin, Tony Morris, Tony Randell, Lisa Smith, Robert Stockdale, Jake Tebbit, Len Jan Vis.

Photographs by Action Plus p60, 83; The Anthony Blake Photo Library p34; Brian Sheul/Collections p8; Coloursport p40; Douglas Dickens p48(l); Morgan/Greenpeace Communications p55; Robert Harding Picture Library p47; Geoff Howard p48(2); The Hulton Deutsch Collection p33; The Hutchison Library p9; The Image Bank p15; Oxford Scientific Films p42; Rex Features p58; Tony Stone Images p6, 12, 20, 31, 38, 48(b), 54(t), 57(m), 58, 62, 64, 67; The Telegraph Colour Library p15; Eye Ubiquitous p6, 44(b), 48(3), 57(t), (b), 58; John Noble/Wilderness Photography p18; Richard Wilkinson p51.

Commissioned photography by Chris Honeywell p14, 15, 16, 42, 44(t), 54.

The authors would like to thank all friends and colleagues especially those at the British Council, Quito 1990–1992 for sharing their life experiences and assisting in the piloting of material. They would also like to thank Philip Prowse, Sarah Comley, Sue Jones, Catherine Smith, Celia Bingham and all the staff at Heinemann ELT for their support.

The publishers would like to thank Calor Gas Limited, Cathay Pacific, Bates Dorland, Ted Edwards, Electrolux, Manjula Goonawardena, Iberia, KLM, Jon Knight, JAL, Quantas, Viasa and Jane Walwyn.

The authors and publishers would like to thank the following for permission to reproduce their material: British Tourist Authority for extracts from 'Britain Information'; Thames & Hudson for extracts from 'The customs and ceremonies of Britian' by Charles Knightly; Covent Garden Market Group for 'Covent Garden Market guide'; Lonely Planet Publications for extracts from 'Ecuador and The Galapagos Islands – A travel survival kit' by Rob Racchowiechi; Liz Driscoll for 'The Singer not the Song'; Options Magazine for 'One big happy family' by Arabella Warner; Anthoney Sheil Associates and John Fowles for extracts from 'The Collector'; Wetherby Arts Festival Committee for 'Ted Edwards the Camel Man'; Random Century Group Ltd for 'Whale Nation' by Heathcote Williams; The Guardian/Reuters for 'Police find crocodile in historian's bath'; Curtis Brown for extracts from 'Quest for adventure' by Chris Bonnington.

While every effort has been made to trace the owners of copyright material in this book, there have been some cases when the publishers have been unable to contact the owners. We should be grateful to hear from anyone who recognises their copyright material and who is unacknowledged. We shall be pleased to make the necessary amendments in future editions of this book.

Printed in Scotland by Cambus Litho

98 99 00 01 10 9 8 7 6 5 4 3 2

Contents

Map of the book

Map of the book

	Language focus	Skills focus
Unit 1 *Tradition*		
Lesson 1 Family celebrations Finding out about family celebrations in different countries	Prepositions of time Present simple	**Reading** for specific information **Speaking** and **writing:** interviewing
Lesson 2 Festivals Finding out about festivals in different countries	Present simple passive	**Reading** for specific information **Writing:** taking notes
Lesson 3 Customs Talking about customs in different countries	Present continuous Present continuous for the future	**Speaking:** discussing **Writing** an informal letter
Unit 2 *Sell it to me*		
Lesson 1 Where to go Planning a shopping trip	*Wh-* questions Countable and uncountable nouns	**Reading** and **listening** for specific information
Lesson 2 Mail order shopping Describing things to buy	Order of adjectives *Yes/No* questions	**Reading** for specific information **Speaking:** the *twenty questions* game
Lesson 3 Advertisements The language of advertisements	First conditional Comparative adjectives	**Listening** for detail **Writing** an advertisement
Unit 3 *Islands*		
Lesson 1 Which island? Describing an island and what it is like to live there	Superlative adjectives Definite and indefinite articles	**Reading** for main idea **Listening** for detail
Lesson 2 Survival at sea A true story about survival in the Pacific Ocean	Past simple Pronunciation of regular verbs in the past simple	**Reading:** ordering a text **Speaking:** speculating
Lesson 3 Skeleton Island Describing the features of an island	Prepositions of place Future with *going to*	**Speaking:** an information gap activity **Listening** for specific information
Unit 4 *Storytelling*		
Lesson 1 '... our dream's come true' Picture story: part 1	Present perfect simple *for* and *since*	**Reading** and **listening** for detail **Speaking:** roleplaying a conversation
Lesson 2 Cindy's crisis Picture story: part 2	*Should* for advice *have got to* for obligation	**Listening** for detail **Writing** an informal letter
Lesson 3 'I can't live without your love' Picture story: part 3	*will* for predictions Pronouns and possessive adjectives and pronouns	**Reading** and **listening** for detail **Writing** a song
Unit 5 *Family life*		
Lesson 1 What size family? Talking about large and small families	Zero conditional Talking about advantages and disadvantages	**Reading** a magazine article **Speaking:** discussing advantages and disadvantages
Lesson 2 House rules Childhood rules and punishments	*be allowed* and *could* for permission *have to* for obligation	**Speaking:** talking about family life **Listening** for specific information
Lesson 3 Family roles Comparing traditional family roles in different countries	Adverbs of frequency	**Speaking:** discussing family roles; interviewing **Listening** for specific information

	Language focus	Skills focus
Unit 6 *Time*		
Lesson 1 Murder at Château Firenze A murder mystery story	Past continuous and past simple *anybody, nobody, somebody, everybody*	**Reading** and **listening** for specific information **Speaking:** speculating
Lesson 2 Time capsules Pyramids and other time capsules	Past simple passive Determiners: *some, a, an*	**Reading** and **listening** for specific information
Lesson 3 The Olympic Games Facts about the games and a general knowledge quiz	Direct and indirect *Wh-* questions	**Reading** and **listening** for specific information **Writing** questions
Unit 7 *Collectors' items*		
Lesson 1 An unusual collection A collection of objects from airplanes and talking about travel experiences	Present perfect and past simple *already, yet* and *just*	**Speaking:** talking about collections and travel experiences **Listening** for specific information
Lesson 2 Collecting information Finding out about market research and conducting a class survey	Present perfect simple and present perfect continuous Polite requests	**Listening** for main idea **Writing:** conducting a survey and writing up notes
Lesson 3 'The Collector' Reading an extract from a novel	*-ing* form	**Reading** a narrative **Speaking:** roleplaying a police interview
Unit 8 *A week of entertainment*		
Lesson 1 What's on? Choosing what to go to at a festival	Making and replying to suggestions Stating preferences	**Reading** for specific information **Speaking:** making arrangements
Lesson 2 A celebrity guest An explorer's adventures	Non-defining relative clauses Phrasal verbs	**Listening** for main ideas and detail **Writing** a publicity article
Lesson 3 Choosing a programme Designing a festival programme and brochure	Talking about likes and dislikes Expressing agreement and disagreement	**Speaking:** roleplaying a committee meeting **Writing:** making a festival programme
Unit 9 *The natural world*		
Lesson 1 Whales Finding out about whales	Comparatives with *'as...as'* Revision of comparatives and superlatives Revision of present perfect	**Reading** a factual text for main idea and detail **Listening** to a radio discussion and expressing opinions
Lesson 2 Favourite animals Unusual pets and famous animals	Reported speech *say* and *tell*	**Listening** to and **writing** descriptions of animals **Reading** a newspaper article
Lesson 3 Nature at work Talking about climate and holidays	Short forms Past continuous	**Reading** and **writing** postcards **Listening** for main ideas and detail
Unit 10 *Into the unknown*		
Lesson 1 The Blue Nile Two expeditions down the Nile	*too* and *enough* Past perfect	**Reading** for main ideas and detail **Speaking:** comparing information
Lesson 2 Cycling across the Andes A cycling expedition in South America	*have to* and *must* for obligation Revision of the *-ing* form	**Listening** and **reading** for main ideas and detail **Speaking:** planning an adventure trip
Lesson 3 Organising an expedition Planning an expedition and asking for sponsorship	Revision of future forms: Present continuous, *going to, will, hope to* and *hope (that)*	**Speaking:** discussing and organizing an expedition **Writing** a formal letter

Lesson 1 *Family celebrations*

Language focus: Present simple

Skills focus: Reading for specific information
Speaking and writing: interviewing

1

Look at these photographs of two different family celebrations. Where do you think these celebrations take place? What do they celebrate?

Listen to someone talking about one of the celebrations. Which photograph is she talking about? What helped you to decide? What is the name of the festival? Do you have a similar festival in your country?

2

Weddings are an important time for family celebration all over the world. The pictures and words below are all connected with weddings in Thailand.

Work in pairs and match the pictures with the words. Compare your answers with another pair.

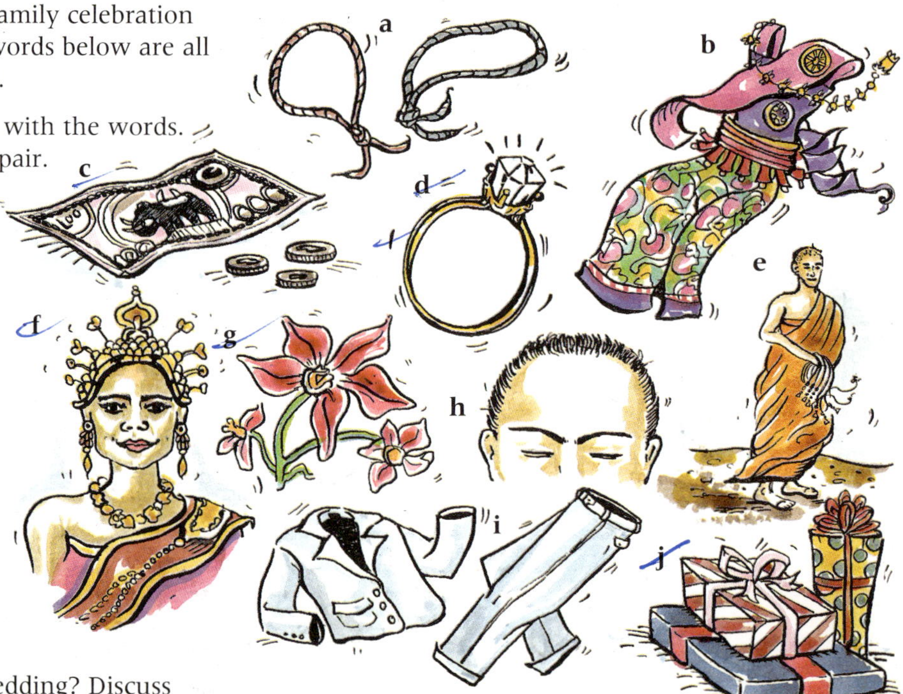

1 bride *picture f*

2 diamond ring d

3 flowers g

4 forehead h (Stirn)

5 money c

6 monk i

7 presents j

Kleidung 8 suit ~~e~~ a e

9 Thai costume b

Faden 10 thread a

What do you think happens at the wedding? Discuss your ideas in groups.

3

Now read the text and see if any of your ideas were correct.

On the wedding day, the bride dresses in traditional Thai costume. The bridegroom usually wears a western-style suit. At lunch-time, the bridegroom goes to the bride's house and the couple prepare an offering of food, flowers and incense. Nine Buddhist monks come to the house and bless the offerings. The actual wedding ceremony takes place at a hotel in the afternoon. The bride and bridegroom sit at a small, low table. The most important person at the wedding, usually the oldest member of the family, places two circles of white thread, joined together over the heads of the bride and bridegroom. Then he or she puts three spots of white powder on their foreheads, for luck. All the wedding guests put water on the hands of the couple and bless them.

Next, there is a party at the hotel with Thai or Chinese food. The couple receive presents of household goods or money from the guests. The bride and bridegroom give each guest a small present. Only the bride wears a ring, usually a diamond, on her left hand.

4

Read the text again and answer these questions.

1 What do the bride and bridegroom wear?

___

2 What do the Buddhist monks do?

___

3 Where does the wedding ceremony take place?

___

4 Who puts the white thread on the couple's heads?

___

5 Why do the bride and bridegroom have three white spots painted on their foreheads?

___

6 What do they eat at the wedding?

___

7 What kind of presents do the couple receive?

___

8 Does the bridegroom wear a ring?

___

5

What things are important for a traditional wedding in your country? Make a list of ten things.

Example

1 - a church
2 - a white dress
3 - a special cake
4

Swap lists with another student and write a question about each item on their list.

Example

1 What happens at the church?
2 Does the bridegroom wear a white dress?
3 What sort of cake do you have?

Now interview your partner and write down their answers.

Example

1 - The wedding ceremony is at the church. There is a priest. All the guests go to the church.
2 - No, he doesn't. He wears a suit.
3 -

6

Work in groups. Tell your group about your partner's list. Answer any questions.

Homework

Write a short paragraph about a family celebration you have in your country.

Language Summary

Prepositions of time
on the wedding day
at lunch-time
in the afternoon

Present simple
The bride **dresses** in traditional Thai costume.
The bridegroom usually **wears** a western-style suit.

see practice page 66

Lesson 2 *Festivals*

Language focus: Present simple passive

Skills focus: Reading for specific information
Writing: taking notes

1

Work in pairs. Look at the photographs of three British festivals. What kind of festival does each photograph show? What time of year do you think they happen?

1

2

3

2

Read the descriptions of the festivals. Match the festivals with the photographs.

A
Egg-rolling takes place on Easter Monday in the north of England. People roll painted boiled eggs down a hill. When the eggs break, they are eaten. This is a pagan custom. Easter (Goddess of Spring) is associated with new life (the egg) and the joy of Spring is shown by the bright colours of the painted eggs.

B
On May 1st in Minehead, a town in south-west England, the Minehead Hobby Horse festival takes place. The hobby horse is a man dressed as a horse and is three or four metres long. At six o'clock in the morning the horse walks one mile west of the town and bows three times to the rising sun. In the afternoon it visits a local castle for drinks and on the second and third of May it visits two towns near Minehead and then returns to dance in the town square. Everywhere it goes money is collected and children are chased by the horse. Originally the Minehead Hobby Horse was thought to bring luck on May Day.

C
The Up-Helly-Aa festival takes place in the Shetland Isles off the north coast of Scotland on January 31st. Up-Helly-Aa marks the end of the Holy Days. At ten o'clock in the morning a ten-metre model of a Viking ship is carried through the town of Lerwick and other villages to the sea. It is followed by the festival chief and forty other men, all dressed in Viking costume. The ship stays there during the day, then at seven o'clock in the evening there is a procession with torches led by the chief and his men through the town to the ship. They throw all the torches onto the ship and it is burnt at sea. Then there are parties and dancing until the next morning.

3

Match the words from the descriptions with their meanings below: a, b, c or d.

A

1 pagan	**a** an important Christian festival
2 associated	**b** non-Christian beliefs
3 Easter	**c** regular habit or tradition
4 custom	**d** connected

B

1 near	**a** bends head forward respectfully
2 bows	**b** coming up
3 chases	**c** close to
4 rising	**d** runs after

C

1 Viking	**a** happens
2 procession	**b** a fighting man from Scandinavia
3 torches	**c** a line of people walking
4 takes place	**d** burning wood which gives light

4

Read the notes in the table about egg-rolling. Make similar notes about the other two festivals and complete the table.

	Egg-rolling	Minehead hobby horse	Up-Helly-Aa
where it takes place	North of England		
when it takes place	Easter Monday		
who participates	adults and children		
why there is a festival	to celebrate Spring		
what happens	people roll painted boiled eggs down a hill. When the eggs break, they eat them.		

5

This is a photograph of another festival. Listen to somebody talking about it.

Where does the festival take place? What does it celebrate?

Now listen again and make notes. Use the headings in Activity 4 to help you.

6

Think about a festival in your town or country and make notes using the same headings as in Activity 4. Then work in groups and tell your group about your festival.

Homework

Write a paragraph about a festival in your town or country.

Language Summary

Present simple passive

When the eggs break, they **are eaten.**

Money **is collected** and children **are chased** by the horse.

see practice page 67

Lesson 3 *Customs*

Language focus: Present continuous

Skills focus: Speaking: discussing
Writing an informal letter

1

Look at the pictures of some things it is rude to do in certain countries. Guess what each picture shows.

Work in pairs and discuss your answers.

Match the pictures with the correct country.

China _picture 2_

India __________

Japan __________

Thailand __________

Now listen to two people talking about the pictures and check your answers.

1

2

3

4

2

Work in pairs. Look at the pictures of some more customs. What are these people doing? Match the pictures below to the activities on the next page.

1

2

3

4

5

6

Activities

a eating with your fingers ____

b taking off your shoes when entering a house ____

c smoking without asking permission ____

d dipping your food in your coffee or tea at breakfast ____

e putting your hand over your mouth when you yawn ____

f arriving early for a party ____

Is it polite or rude to do any of these things in your country?

Mark *P* next to the things that are polite, *R* next to the things that are rude, *N* next to the things that are neither polite nor rude or *U* next to the things that it is unusual to do.

Compare your answers with two other students.

3

What is rude or not polite in your country? What advice about customs could you give a visitor to your country? Think about the following things:

- asking someone how much they earn
- being half an hour late for an appointment
- leaving some food on your plate at the end of a meal
- offering to wash up after a meal
- shaking hands with everyone when you enter a room
- taking flowers with you when you visit someone

Write down as many things as you can think of and compare your list with a partner.

4

Kate is writing a letter to her Japanese friend, Yoshi, who is coming to visit her in Britain. What things does she tell Yoshi to bring?

47 Elm Grove
Southsea
Hampshire

23rd June

Dear Yoshi,

Thank you for your letter. I'm so pleased that you're visiting us next month.

My sister's getting married on the 30th and you're invited. It'll be a formal wedding so bring something smart to wear. It's traditional to give the bride and groom a wedding present but it's not necessary to buy anything expensive.

It often rains here in the summer so don't forget to bring an umbrella!

See you soon,

Love Kate

PS We'll meet you at the airport.

Homework

Write a letter to a friend who is coming to visit your country. Tell him or her about any local customs – things you should do and things it's rude or not polite to do – and describe a local festival or family celebration that will take place during his or her stay.

Language Summary

Present continuous
She's **holding** something in her hand.
Is she **laughing**?

Present continuous for the future
I'm so pleased that you**'re visiting** us next month.

see practice page 68

Lesson 1 *Where to go*

Language focus: *Wh-* questions
Skills focus: Reading and listening for specific information

1

Look at the photograph. Where are the people? What are they doing?

2

Look at the shopping guide to Covent Garden in London and answer the questions.

LOCAL ATTRACTIONS

The London Transport Museum Covent Garden, WC2E 7BB. Tel 071 379 6344. Unique working exhibits, historic vehicles, videos, posters.
Open daily 10am–6pm. Visit the Museum Shop for unusual and attractive souvenirs.

The Theatre Museum Russell Street, WC2. Tel 071 836 7891. The National Museum of the Performing Arts.
Open Tues–Sun 11am–7pm. Café and Box Office open until 8pm. Recorded information 071 836 7624.

Cabaret Mechanical Theatre 33/34 The Market, Covent Garden, WC2E 8RE. Tel 071 379 7961. You will not have seen anything like this anywhere before. Aged 9 months or 99, you can make over 50 mechanical models come to life.
Open Mon–Sun 10am–6.30pm.

RESTAURANTS

Monkey Business 35 The Piazza, Covent Garden WC2. Tel 071 379 5803. An American Bistro and Bar featuring Cajun, Creole and Texx Mex. Dinner dancing.
Open 7 days: Mon–Wed noon–1am, Thurs–Sat noon–2am, Sun noon–10.30pm.

The Italian Connection Strand Palace Hotel, Strand, WC2R 0JJ. Tel 071 836 8080. For delicious pizzas and pastas in a lively atmosphere. £2 discount with this leaflet.
Open for lunch Mon–Fri 12.30pm–2pm and dinner Mon–Sat 5.30pm–midnight.

Ponti's of Covent Garden 5 The Market, WC2. Tel 071 836 0272. Famous for its real Italian cuisine, ice cream and cakes.

Trouts Fish & Chip Restaurant, 11 Henrietta Street, WC2. Tel 071 379 5555.

SPECIALIST SHOPS

Stanfords 12–14 Long Acre, WC2E 9LP. Tel 071 836 1321. The world's best map and travel bookshop with over 10,000 British and Overseas maps and guides. Specialist in OS Maps, Globes, Climbing, Maritime.

SHOPPING

Jubilee Market Hall The Piazza, WC2. Tel 071 836 2139. Jubilee Market offers quality and value for money in its 3 markets on the south side of the Piazza.
Mon antiques, Tue–Fri general goods, Sat–Sun craft fair.

Covent Garden Market Speciality shops, craft and antique stalls, a pub, wine bars, restaurants and a wide range of entertainment, every day from 10am until late.

Royal Opera House Shop James Street, Covent Garden, WC2. Tel 071 240 1200 ext 343. London's best specialist shop for opera and ballet CDs, tapes and videos, posters, T-shirts, libretti and gifts.
Open Mon–Sat 10am–7.30pm. Mail order: ext 217.

Dillons Arts Bookshop 8 Long Acre, WC2E 9LN. Tel 071 836 1359. London's largest arts bookshop. Two floors of books on art, architecture, design, fiction, poetry, drama, film and music.
Open until 10pm Mon–Sat, 12–8pm Sundays.

TRANSPORT INFORMATION

London Transport 24 hour information 071 222 1234.
Underground Stations: Covent Garden: Piccadilly line.
Charing Cross: Bakerloo, Jubilee & Northern lines.
Leicester Square: Piccadilly & Northern lines.

1 Where can you buy travel and guide books? Stanfords

2 You want to eat fish and chips. Where can you go? ________

3 How many shops are open on Sundays? ________

4 What's the phone number of the London Transport Museum? ________

5 Where can you have dinner and dance too? ________

6 How much money can you save at The Italian Connection? ________

7 Where will you find a book about Picasso? ________

8 Who serves real Italian ice cream in Covent Garden? ________

9 How many models are there in the Cabaret Mechanical Theatre? ________

10 When is the craft fair in Jubilee Market Hall? ________

11 Where can you go for a good pizza? ________

12 When can you phone for London Transport information? ________

13 How many hours a day does the Theatre Museum open? ________

14 Which shop sells ballet videos? ________

15 Where can you buy antiques? ________

Compare your answers with another student.

3

Look at the Covent Garden guide again and listen to these four conversations. Where are the people? What helped you to decide?

1 ________________________

2 ________________________

3 ________________________

4 ________________________

4

Work in groups. You have two hours in Covent Garden. Choose four places to visit. Tell another group why you made your choices.

Example

We want to go to Trouts for lunch because we like fish and chips.

5

What kind of shops do you have in your town, or the town where you are studying?

Write six questions asking for information. Use the questions in Activity 2 to help you.

Example

How many shops are open on Sundays?
Where can you go for a good pizza?

Work in groups of four. Can anyone in your group answer your questions? Can you answer any of their questions?

Homework

Write a short guide to shopping in your town, or the town where you are studying. Use the Covent Garden guide and the questions and information you collected in Activity 6 to help you. Go into the town and find out more if necessary. Include shops and restaurants in your description.

Language Summary

Wh- questions
Where can you buy the best travel books?
When is the craft fair in Jubilee Market Hall?

Countable and uncountable nouns
How many shops are open on Sundays?
How much money can you save at The Italian Connection?

see practice page 69

Lesson 2 *Mail order shopping*

Language focus: Order of adjectives
Skills focus: Reading for specific information
Speaking: The *twenty questions* game

1

Match the items with the catalogue descriptions.

1 Indian silk and cotton waistcoat. Available in one design only in red. Large size fits everybody. **£22.95**.

2 Pocket-sized calculator. Multi-function with memory, black plastic. Made in Japan. **£12.99**.

3 Multicoloured glass jewellery. From Africa. Necklace **£6.95**.

4 Blue and white ceramic vase. The perfect present. Chinese design. Beautifully painted. 50cm high. **£71.00**.

5 Italian leather belt. In brown or black. Small (60–71cm), medium (71–81cm) and large (81–97cm). For men and women. **£23.99**.

6 Matching suitcases. Medium and large. For all your travel needs. Made in Canada in strong canvas with leather handles. Dark green only with light brown leather. Only **£119.99**.

1 ___f___ 2 ______ 3 ______
4 ______ 5 ______ 6 ______

Which would you like to buy for yourself?

Which would you like to buy for someone you know?

2

Look at the descriptions again. Find words in the descriptions to complete the table.

size	colour	origin	material	noun
large		Indian	silk and cotton	waistcoat

3

Now write catalogue descriptions for these three objects using some of the adjectives in Activity 2.

What is your favourite possession? Write a description for it. Why is it important to you?

Homework

Choose two things you bought recently (or would like to buy) and write descriptions of them. Use the descriptions in Activity 1 to help you.

4

Listen to some people playing the *twenty questions* game. What object are they talking about?

Now *you* play the game. One person thinks of an object you can find in a house. The other students in the class can only ask 20 yes/no questions to find out what it is.

Example

Is it made of plastic?

No

Do you use it in the bathroom?

Yes

Language Summary

Order of adjectives

Indian silk and cotton waistcoat.

Multicoloured glass jewellery from Africa.

Yes/No questions

Is it made of plastic?

Do you use it in the bathroom?

see practice page 70

Lesson 3 *Advertisements*

Language focus: First conditional
Skills focus: Listening for detail
Writing an advertisement

1

2

3

1

Work in pairs. Look at the photographs from some advertisements. What do you think they are advertising? Choose a, b, or c for each advertisement.

Example

I think 1 is an aquarium.

I don't. I think it's b, a garden centre.

1 **a** an aquarium
b gas central heating
c a garden centre

2 **a** paint
b a dishwasher
c a home security company

3 **a** a new supermarket
b clothes for tall and short people
c a health club

2

Match the products below to the correct slogan.

1 low fat margarine
2 deodorant
3 chocolate
4 washing up liquid
5 language centre
6 washing powder
7 alarm clock

a Get a bigger bar!
b The more reliable way to be on time every day!
c Gets your clothes cleaner!
d Keeps you drier round the clock!
e The healthier alternative to butter!
f Softer for your hands and dishes!
g Learn English the easier way!

Which words helped you to decide which product matched each slogan?

3

What will happen if you use or buy the products in Activity 2? Write sentences.

Make up a name for each product.

Example

If you eat Garden Farm low fat margarine, you will be healthier.
or
You will be healthier if you eat Garden Farm low fat margarine.

4

Listen to these radio advertisements and complete the table.

Name of shop/company	What is being advertised	Selling points
1 African Experience Wildlife Park	a day out	more interesting wider variety of animals
2 Hobson's		
3 Sunshine Company		

Homework

Choose a product you have at home or one from a magazine and write your own radio advertisement.

5

You are going to listen to another radio advertisement. First, try and complete the gaps using the comparative adjectives from the selling points in the table in Activity 4.

Woodbridge Sport and Leisure Centre offers you a (1) *more interesting* way to spend your leisure time with an even (2) ______________ selection of sports facilities than you can imagine. Try squash, badminton, indoor tennis and football or attend one of our exercise classes – we have a (3) ______________ variety, all with fully-qualified instructors. We also have facilities for (4) ______________ sports such as scuba diving and rock climbing. Now that summer's here and the weather is (5) ______________, why not swim in our outdoor pool? If you want a (6) ______________ way to spend your free time, you will find something here at Woodbridge Sport and Leisure Centre. We have a (7) ______________ choice of sports all at (8) ______________ prices than our competitors. Woodbridge Sports and Leisure Centre, just off the A10 south of Woodbridge. See you there!

Now listen to the advertisement and check your answers.

6

Work in pairs. Write a radio advertisement for a place of interest in your town, or find an advertisement you like from a newspaper or magazine and write a radio advertisement for the product.

Language Summary

First conditional

If you **eat** Garden Farm low fat margarine, you **will be** healthier.
or
You **will be** healthier **if** you **eat** Garden Farm low fat margarine.

Comparative adjectives

Now that summer is here and the weather is **sunnier**.
Aways wanted to go somewhere **more exciting** than Europe?

see practice page 71

Lesson 1 *Which island?*

Language focus: Superlative adjectives

Skills focus: Reading for main idea
Listening for detail

1

Look at the outlines of the islands and match them with the names.

Japan	Britain	Crete
Iceland	New Zealand	The Galapagos

1 ______________

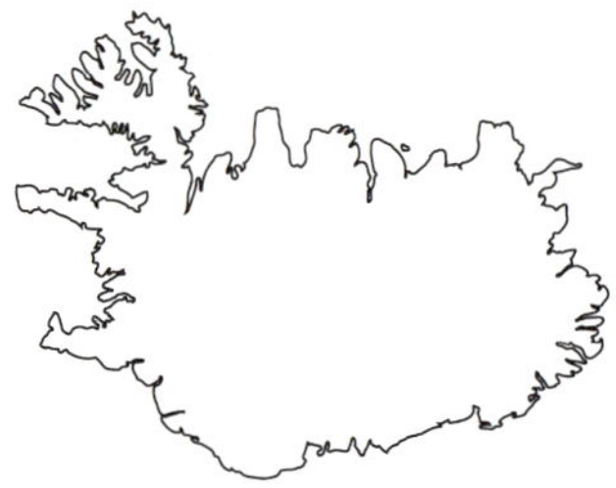

2 ______________

3 *Britain*

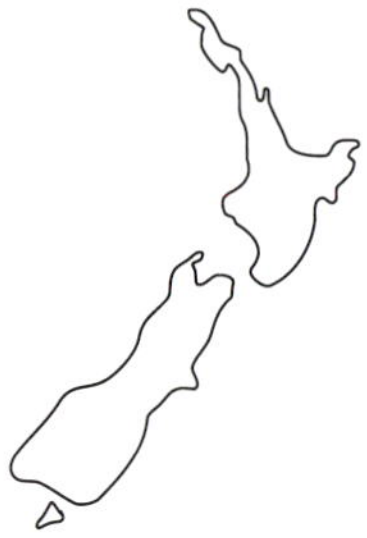

4 ______________

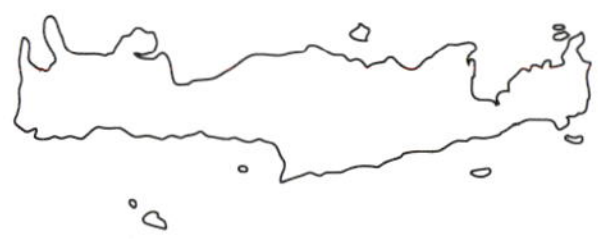

5 ______________

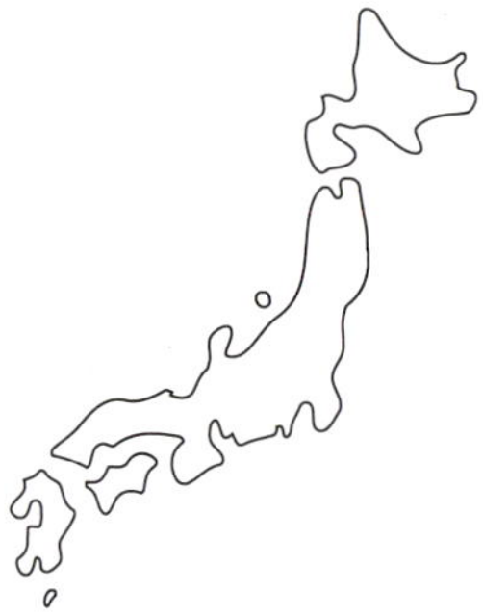

6 ______________

Where are these islands? Match the islands to the locations. Look at a map if necessary.

1 In South America, west of Ecuador. *The Galapagos*
2 In Europe, south of the Greek mainland. ______________
3 In northern Europe, west of Scandinavia. ______________
4 In Far East Asia, east of China. ______________
5 In Europe, north-west of France. ______________
6 In Asia, south-east of Australia. ______________

2

Read the text about the Galapagos Islands. Are these statements true or false?

1 The islands were discovered in the 16th century.
2 Charles Darwin gave the islands their name.
3 The islands are a national park.
4 The islands are near the mainland.
5 There are volcanoes on the islands.
6 Not all of the islands are inhabited.
7 It is not expensive to visit the islands.

1 The Galapagos are an isolated group of volcanic islands on the equator, 1,000 km west of Ecuador. There are thirteen big islands and six smaller ones in the group and many tiny islets. Five of the islands are inhabited with a population of about 9,000 people who make a living mainly from tourism, fishing and farming. Santa Cruz is the second largest island in the Galapagos. It has the largest population because all the tourism is here.

2 A Bishop from Panama discovered the Galapagos islands in 1535. The Bishop named the islands after the galapagos, the giant tortoises which live there. The tortoises provided fresh meat for sailors, pirates and seal and whale hunters who used the islands as a base for the next three centuries.

3 Charles Darwin visited the islands in 1835 and stayed for five weeks, making notes about the wildlife. Ecuador officially claimed the islands in 1832 and the Galapagos became a national park in 1959.

4 The islands are famous for their incredible wildlife and beautiful scenery. The Galapagos are a very popular tourist destination – 20,000 people visited in 1993 – but only if you have a lot of money! It is one of the most expensive places in the world to visit, because of the airfare from the mainland and the cost of the holiday cruises round the islands.

3

Look at the text again. What information does each paragraph give you? Write the paragraph number next to the information.

tourist information *4*

early history ______

geography and population ______

why the islands are famous ______

industries ______

how the islands got their name ______

recent history ______

Homework

Think about the islands in Activity 1. Which island do you think is the coldest, the hottest, the wettest, the most expensive, the cheapest, the sunniest, the most isolated? Write seven sentences.

4

You are going to hear Sheika González, a naturalist guide on the island of Santa Cruz, describing her life on the Galapagos islands.

Which of these words do you think you will hear?

aeroplane bus cinema cities coffee education electricity generator fresh water nature newspaper radio station sunshine swimming toothbrush umbrella wind

Listen to Sheika and check your predictions.

5

Work in pairs. What are the advantages of living on the islands? What are the disadvantages?

Listen again and make notes.

6

Write a short description of an island or remote place in your country. What are the advantages and disadvantages of living there? Think about education, transport and entertainment.

Use Activities 2 and 3 to help you.

Language Summary

Superlative adjectives

Santa Cruz is **the** second **largest** island in the Galapagos.
The Galapagos are one of **the most expensive** places in the world to visit.

Definite and indefinite articles

The Galapagos are **an** isolated group of volcanic islands on **the** Equator.
A Bishop from Panama discovered **the** Galapagos islands in 1535.

see practice page 72

Lesson 2 *Survival at sea*

Language focus: Past simple
Skills focus: Reading: ordering a text
Speaking: speculating

1

This is a true story about the Robertson family.

Read the text and match the drawings with the words in the box.

In 1971 the Robertsons decided to sail around the world. They sold their farm and house and bought a yacht called 'The Lucette'. This is the first part of the story of their adventures.

At 9.55 am on 15th June, 1972, killer whales attacked 'The Lucette'. The whales made holes in the yacht and water started to come in. 'The Lucette' was 250 km south west of the Galapagos islands and was carrying the Robertson family – Dougal Robertson, his wife Lyn, their twin sons Sandy and Neil, aged 11, another son, Douglas, aged 17, and a friend, Robin, a 22-year-old student.

Quickly, they all got into the life raft and took the rowing boat from the yacht too. Four minutes later 'The Lucette' sank. All the group had with them was a first aid box, eight flares, twelve onions, ten oranges, six lemons, half a kilo of biscuits, some sweets and no clothes other than swimming shorts and shirts.

~~flare~~ killer whale life raft rowing boat
sail shark turtle yacht

1 turtle

2 shark

3 life raft

4 killer whale

5 yacht

6 *flare*

7 rowing boat

8 sail

2

Look at the passage again and answer the questions.

1 Why did 'The Lucette' sink? Killer whales made holes in the yacht

2 How many people were there on the yacht? 6

3 What food did they have? 12 onions 10 oranges ½kg biscuits some sweets

3

The group survived at sea for 37 days. Work in pairs and answer these questions.

- How do you think they survived?
- What did they eat and drink?
- How did they get their food and water?
- What problems do you think they had?
- What do you think happened to them?

Discuss your answers with another pair.

4

The sentences below tell the rest of the story but they are not in the right order. Put them in the correct order and find out what happened to the group. Write your answers in the boxes below.

1	2	3	4	5	6	7	8	9	10	11
j	f	k	g	c	a	d	i	e	h	b

a Sharks smelt the turtle blood and came to the boats. From then on sharks followed them all the time.
b A Japanese fishing boat saw the flare and rescued them. They were 600 miles off the coast of Panama.
c On Day 7, Douglas killed a turtle so they had ten kilos of meat, which they dried in the sun.
d They had been on the life raft for two weeks. It had lots of holes in it and was always wet. So on Day 17 they moved into the rowing boat, which was drier.
e They were very short of drinking water after the storm.
f At first Robin and Neil were seasick. Luckily Lyn was a nurse, so she knew which pills to give them from the first aid box.
g When they had no more lemons, they ate raw fish.
h On Day 38 Dougal saw a ship coming towards them and lit a flare.
i After they moved into the rowing boat, there was a very bad storm.
j They quickly decided that the rowing boat was going to pull the boat they were in, so they put up a sail.
k On Day 3 Sandy caught their first fish. They cut it up and put it in the lemon juice which 'cooked' it.

Listen to the tape and check your answers.

5

Look at these adjectives which we can use to describe feelings. Write **+** next to the adjectives which are positive and **–** next to the adjectives which are negative. Use a dictionary if necessary.

comfortable	+	confident	+	depressed	___
excited	+	frightened	___	happy	+
lonely	___	relieved	+	thirsty	___
tired	___	uncomfortable	___	worried	___

How do you think the people in the story felt during their adventure?

Work in groups. Choose six sentences from the jumbled story in Activity 4. For each sentence you have chosen, write another sentence saying how the people on 'The Lucette' felt during their adventure.

Example

Sentence e: They were thirsty because they were very short of drinking water after the storm.

Compare your sentences with another group.

Homework

Imagine you are one of the people on 'The Lucette'. Write a paragraph in your diary saying how you felt on that day of your adventure.

Language Summary

Past simple

In 1971 the Robertsons **decided** to sail around the world. They **sold** their farm and house and **bought** a yacht called 'The Lucette'.

Pronunciation of regular verbs in the past simple
/d/, /t/, /ɪd/

see practice page 73

Lesson 3 *Skeleton Island*

Language focus: Prepositions of place

Skills focus: Speaking: an information gap activity
Listening for specific information

1

Work in pairs. Write the words in the box next to the correct pictures in the key.

beach crocodiles jungle mountains
piranha river skeleton snakes
swamp ~~volcano~~

2

Look at the map of Skeleton Island.

Listen to Part 1 of a description of the island. Decide if the statements are true or false. Correct the ones that are false.

1 *False. The snakes are near the beach.*
2 ______
3 ______
4 ______
5 ______
6 ______
7 ______

Now listen to Part 2 of the description and complete the map.

Compare your answers with your partner.

3

Work in pairs. Look at the blank map of the island. First, give your island a name. Then each choose five different things from the key in Activity 1 and draw them on your map. Do not look at your partner's map or let him/her see yours.

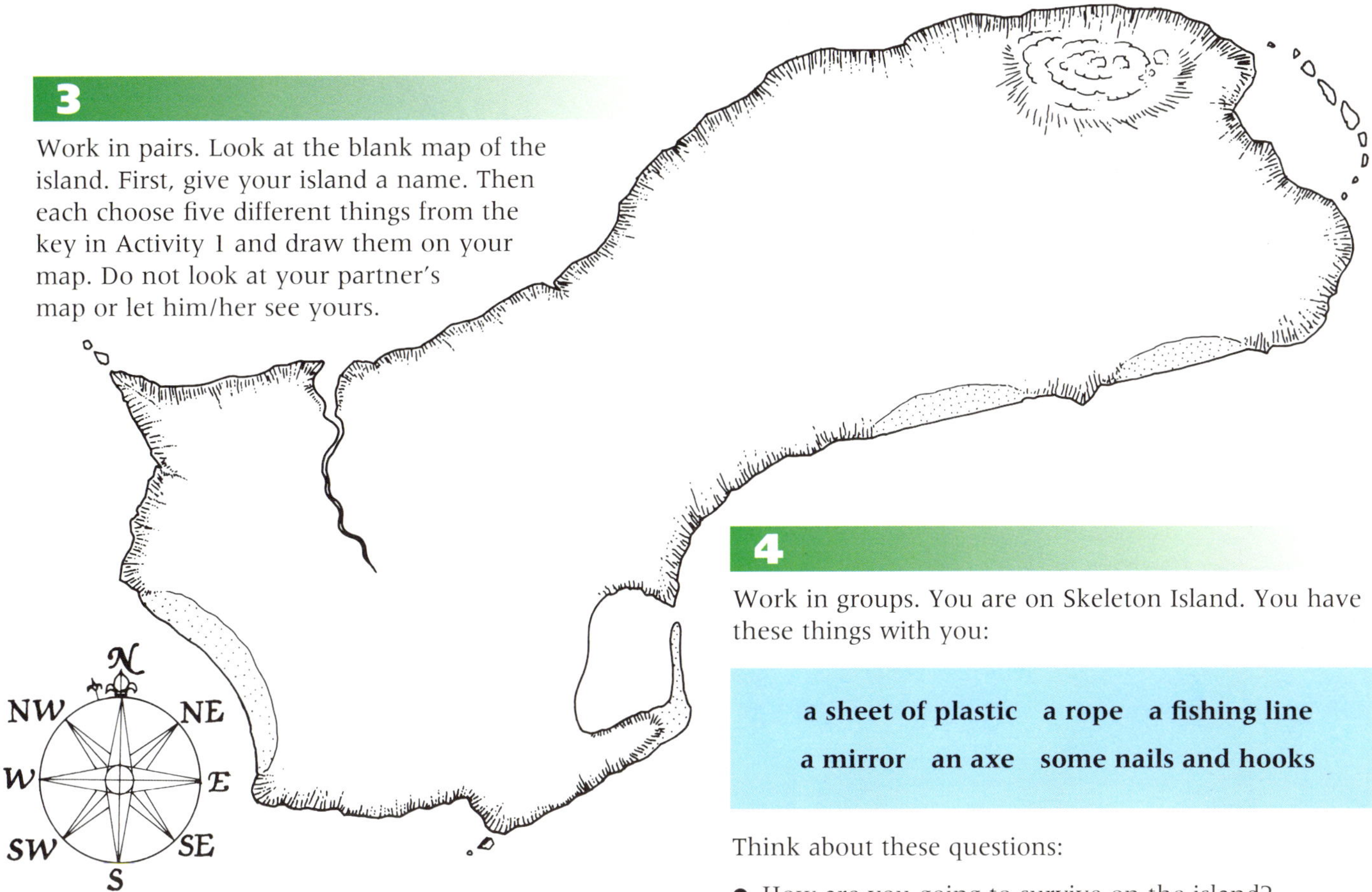

Take it in turns to ask each other questions about your partner's island and draw on your map the things your partner describes.

Examples

Student A
Is there a volcano on your island?

Student B
Yes, there is.

Student A
Where's the volcano?

Student B
It's in the centre of the island.

When you have finished compare your maps.

Homework

You are alone on your island. Write your diary for three days. Describe what happened and how you felt.

4

Work in groups. You are on Skeleton Island. You have these things with you:

a sheet of plastic   a rope   a fishing line
a mirror   an axe   some nails and hooks

Think about these questions:

- How are you going to survive on the island?
- What are you going to eat?
- Which part of the island are you going to live on?
- How are you going to escape?

Report your plans back to the class.

Example

We're going to live in the north of the island.

We're going to catch fish to eat.

Language Summary

Prepositions of place
The sharks are **at** South Point.
The volcano is **in the centre of** the island.

Future with *going to*
We'**re going to live** in the north of the island.
We'**re going to catch** fish to eat.

see practice page 74

Lesson 1 *'... our dream's come true'*

Language focus: Present perfect simple

Skills focus: Reading and listening for detail
Speaking: roleplaying a conversation

1

Do you like pop music? Have you got a favourite band or song? Does anyone else in the class like the same as you?

2

Read the first part of the story *The singer not the song* and answer the questions.

So Tony went over to Brock's office to sign the contract. When Tony left, Cindy and Rob started working again. Cindy picked up her guitar. Why was she so nervous when she was alone with Rob? Tony was so enthusiastic about everything. She didn't feel nervous with him. She liked Rob too. But why was he always so serious?

1 What's the name of the band? How many people are there in the band and what are their names?
2 Cindy says 'We've always wanted this chance'. What is the chance?
3 Where does Tony go? Why?
4 Does Cindy prefer Rob or Tony? How do you know?
5 How does Rob feel about Cindy? How do you know?

3

What do you think happens next? Discuss your ideas in groups.

Listen to the next part of the story and check your predictions.

4

Work in pairs. Read the summary. There are some factual mistakes in it. Underline the differences.

Listen again to check.

Rob has liked Cindy since he met her, but she isn't interested in him. The band has been the most important thing in Cindy's life for a long time. Rob signed the contract and the band are going to the studio on Friday at 10 am to record their song. On Tuesday they meet at Tony's flat. Tony's sister Lucy is there too. The song is perfect. Lucy tells Cindy that Rob has been unhappy for weeks because of her. Rob and Lucy go out to get some Italian food, and Tony and Cindy listen to Mozart. Lucy comes back without Rob and tells Tony something. They both look happy.

5

What do you think has happened? Work in groups of three and roleplay the conversation between Tony, Cindy and Lucy.

Homework

Write your conversation from Activity 5.

Language Summary

Present perfect simple

We'**ve worked** together for five years now.
The band **has been** the most important thing in Cindy's life for a long time.

for and *since*

We've only worked on my new song **for** two days.
We've wanted to make a record **since** we started the band.

see practice page 75

Lesson 2 *Cindy's crisis*

Language focus: *should* for advice

Skills focus: Listening for detail
Writing an informal letter

1

What has happened in the story so far? Work in pairs and tell your partner what you can remember.

2

Listen to the next part of the story. Are these sentences true or false?

1 Rob's had an accident. _T_
2 He didn't look when he crossed the road. ___
3 A lorry hit him. ___
4 He's in hospital. ___
5 He's dead. ___
6 Tony loves Cindy. ___
7 Tony and Cindy go to the recording studio on Thursday. ___
8 Two months later, Cindy feels fine again. ___

3

Read the next part of the story. What advice does Lucy give Cindy? Is it good advice?

4

What do you think Cindy should do? Work with a partner and think of some advice to give her.

Example

I think Cindy should take a holiday.

She shouldn't stay at home all the time.

Homework

You are Cindy's sister. Write a reply to the letter you wrote in Activity 6.

5

Now find out what Cindy decides to do. Listen to the next part of the story and put the events in the correct order.

- **a** Cindy met Tony the next day.
- **b** Tony kissed Cindy.
- **c** Cindy remembered her last conversation with Rob.
- **d** Cindy told Tony 'I can't sing without Rob.'
- **e** Cindy started to cry.
- **f** Cindy listened to Rob's last song.
- **g** Cindy ran into her flat.
- **h** Tony told Cindy 'I'll find another person for the band.'

1	2	3	4	5	6	7	8

6

Cindy wrote a letter to her sister telling what happened and asking for advice. Write Cindy's letter.

Language Summary

should for advice

I think Cindy **should** take a holiday.
She **shouldn't** stay at home all the time.

have got to for obligation

You'**ve got to** start living again.
You'**ve got to** help Tony.

see practice page 76

Lesson 3 *'I can't live without your love'*

Language focus: *will* for predictions

Skills focus: Reading and listening for detail
Writing a song

1

Look at the next part of the picture story. Match the speech and thought bubbles with the correct picture and the correct person.

1 I can't live without your love.

2 Cindy doesn't want to sing again. That's what she said. Perhaps she'll change her mind and help Tony now.

3 Is Tony's concert tonight or tomorrow night?

4 You've got to go out more Cindy. Staying at home all the time isn't good for you.

5 It's tonight. It starts at 9.00 o'clock. Poor Tony – he'll be so nervous.

6 Yes, and he's got a real problem with one song. He just can't get it right. It's Rob's last song – you know the one he wrote before he ...

7 Oh, that's good. I'm really pleased for him. But he'll be nervous on his own.

8 Not too bad. He's going on tour next month – to Manchester, Liverpool and Birmingham.

Now listen to the story and check your anwers.

2

How do you think the story will end? Discuss in groups.

Now listen to the last part of the story. Were you right?

3

What do you think will happen now? Think about Cindy and Tony in five years' time. Will they make another record? Will they be successful? Discuss your ideas in groups.

4

Work in groups. Write the words of a new song for Cindy and Tony's band, Duo.

Homework

Write a short dialogue between Brock, the agent, and the record company Sound Nation. They are talking about Tony's new band, Duo. Start it like this:

Brock: I think we really have something big here I was at the concert last night and Duo were great ...

Language Summary

will for predictions

He'**ll** be nervous on his own.

Cindy **won't** change her mind.

Pronouns and possessive adjectives and pronouns

I'm really pleased for **him**.

I can't live without **your** love.

see practice page 77

Lesson 1 *What size family?*

Language focus: Zero conditional

Skills focus: Reading a magazine article
Speaking: discussing advantages and disadvantages

1

Look at the picture of Richard and Janet Aston and their eight children.

Read the description of the five daughters and find them in the picture.

1 Kate has got long blonde wavy hair. She's wearing jeans and a jumper. _b_
2 Victoria has got long blonde hair too, but she's wearing a skirt and a shirt. ___
3 Emily has got short brown hair. She's wearing jeans and a shirt. ___
4 Elizabeth has got a round face and dark wavy hair. She's wearing a track suit and a jacket. ___
5 Sarah is tall and has got a long face. Her eyes and hair are dark and she wears glasses. She's wearing jeans and a jumper. ___

2

Work in pairs. Look at the adjectives to describe character below. Write + next to the adjectives which are positive and – next to the adjectives which are negative. Which adjectives can be both positive and negative? Use a dictionary if necessary.

bored ___	careful ___	fair ___
hard-working ___	imaginative ___	lazy ___
lonely ___	noisy ___	quiet ___
spoilt ___	strict ___	

Now read the article about the Astons. Which adjectives describe Richard, Janet, Sarah and Victoria?

Read the text again and answer the following questions:

- Who have bedrooms of their own? ___________
- Who was an only child? ___________

JANET puts the reason for her large family down to the fact that she was an only child: 'Life was so lonely and dull for me I knew I wanted lots of children.' But there are difficulties. If they go anywhere as a family they need two cars. And big families have big appetites. The Astons consume ten pints of milk and two loaves of bread a day. They also produce a lot of washing – four loads a day.

Richard is an accountant and budgets carefully for everything. The phone is his main worry – the children spend too long on it. Nor can they afford to go abroad on holiday. The eldest children work and Janet works part-time in a doctor's surgery.

Another problem is that you get no privacy or space. Janet and Richard share their room with the two youngest Astons, and Emily and Elizabeth sleep in the same bed so that Christopher and Sarah can have rooms of their own. 'That doesn't mean that you get left alone though,' complained Sarah. 'My room is on the ground floor, and if I bring a friend home, I get five faces at the window.'

Although Richard and Janet are great believers in fairness, it often doesn't work out in practice. Christopher claims that his parents were stricter with the older children, and that Victoria never does any work. Although the children may complain about each other and say that they won't have large families themselves, there is a general

understanding that being part of a large family is something special. 'My friends love listening to all the stories about us,' said Sarah. 'Most people have such boring lives compared to ours.'

3

Work in groups. What are the advantages and disadvantages of living in a large family? Make notes using the text to help you.

Example

advantages	*disadvantages*
never boring	*expensive*

Homework

Write down four advantages and four disadvantages of being an only child.

Example

One advantage of being an only child is that you get lots of presents.
One disadvantage of being an only child is that you can be lonely.

4

Read Debra's statements below. Do you think she is from a large or small family?

'I was bored.'

'I used to have a lot of imaginary brothers and sisters.'

'I didn't have to share a bedroom.'

'I got lots of presents.'

'I was very spoilt.'

'Lots of fuss was made over me.'

'Now my parents are older, the responsibility will be all mine.'

'My parents talked to me a lot.'

Now listen to Debra talking about her family life and tick the points she mentions. Which adjectives in Activity 2 do you think describe Debra?

5

Work in groups. Which of Debra's and the Astons' experiences happened to you? What do you think is the ideal number of children to have? Give your reasons.

Language Summary

Zero conditional

If they **go** anywhere as a family, they **need** two cars.
If I **bring** a friend home, I **get** five faces at the window.

Talking about advantages and disadvantages

One advantage of being an only child **is that** you get lots of presents.
One disadvantage of being an only child **is that** you can be very lonely.

see practice page 78

Lesson 2 *House rules*

Language focus: *be allowed* and *could* for permission; *have to* for obligation

Skills focus: Speaking: talking about family life
Listening for specific information

1

Look at these family rules for children. Tick (✓) the ones you agree with and cross (✗) the ones you disagree with. Did you have any of these rules in your family?

- ☐ No smoking.
- ☐ No eating snacks or sweets between meals.
- ☐ No playing with children in the street.
- ☐ No swearing.
- ☐ Always having to ask for permission to go out.
- ☐ Having to do your homework every evening.
- ☐ Having to eat all your dinner.
- ☐ Always coming home on time.
- ☐ Having to make your bed every day.

Work in pairs and compare your answers.

Examples

I was allowed to drink wine at dinner, but I wasn't allowed to smoke.

I could eat sweets between meals, and I didn't have to eat all my dinner.

2

Now look at some possible punishments for breaking the rules. Tick the ones you agree with and cross the ones you disagree with. Did any of these things happen to you?

- ☐ You have to go to bed.
- ☐ You have to stay in your room.
- ☐ You are not allowed to have any sweets.
- ☐ Your parents hit you.
- ☐ Your parents shout at you.
- ☐ You can't have any dinner.
- ☐ You can't watch TV.
- ☐ You have to clean the house.
- ☐ You have to eat cold/old food.
- ☐ You are not allowed to go out.

Work in pairs. Compare your answers and give your reasons.

Examples

Yes, I had to go to bed when I didn't eat my dinner – I disagree with that.

I didn't have to clean the house, but I had to clean my room. I think that's a good punishment.

3

Listen to Jane and Brendan talking about the house rules they had when they were young. Write J next to the rules from Activity 1 that Jane mentions, and B next to the ones Brendan mentions.

Did Jane and Brendan think having strict parents was a good thing?

4

Work in groups. Look at the photograph of Jane when she was a teenager. Where do you think she is? What kind of clothes do you think she is wearing? How do you think she is feeling?

You are going to hear a story from Jane's past. First, try to guess what happened using the photograph and the words in the box.

father fire hippie lam
rock festival shopping

Listen and check your predictions.

5

Did you ever break the rules when you were a child? Work in pairs. Tell your partner what you did and what happened to you.

Homework

Write a paragraph about one occasion when you broke some house rules.

Language Summary

be allowed and *could* for permission
I **was allowed** to drink wine at dinner
but I **wasn't allowed** to smoke.
I **could** eat sweets between meals.

have to for obligation
I **didn't have to** clean the house,
but I **had to** clean my room.

see practice page 79

Lesson 3 *Family roles*

Language focus: Adverbs of frequency

Skills focus: Speaking: discussing family roles; interviewing
Listening for specific information

1

Look at the following statements. Which do you agree with? Which do you disagree with? Number your answers: 1 – agree strongly, 2 – agree, 3 – neutral, 4 – disagree, 5 – disagree strongly.

- ☐ You shouldn't have children if you're not married.
- ☐ Marriage between people from different cultures is always difficult.
- ☐ Unmarried couples living together is wrong.
- ☐ It is too easy to divorce these days.
- ☐ The oldest child should look after the parents when they are old.
- ☐ A child always needs a mother AND a father.
- ☐ People often spend too much money on weddings.
- ☐ Single parents should get help from the government.
- ☐ Men don't usually spend enough time with their children.
- ☐ You shouldn't have more than one child.

2

What are family customs in Italy like? Work in groups and write down your ideas.

Listen to Ida, who is Italian, and number the topics below in the order she talks about them.

- ☐ children
- ☐ divorce
- ☐ living together
- ☐ marriage
- ☐ old relatives
- ☐ role of the father
- ☐ role of the mother
- ☐ single parents

3

What does Ida say about family customs? Listen again. Complete the sentences below and tick a, b or c in the boxes under Ida.

	Ida	Jan
1 The father		
a usually goes out to work.	☐	☐
b often stays at home.	☐	☐
c always goes out to work.	☐	☐
2 The mother		
a never goes out to work.	☐	☐
b often goes out to work.	☐	☐
c usually stays at home.	☐	☐
3 Children have		
a a lot of freedom.	☐	☐
b limited freedom.	☐	☐
c no freedom.	☐	☐
4 Living together		
a is common.	☐	☐
b never happens.	☐	☐
c is difficult.	☐	☐
5 Marriage is		
a unpopular.	☐	☐
b popular.	☐	☐
c expensive.	☐	☐
6 Divorce		
a often happens.	☐	☐
b sometimes happens.	☐	☐
c never happens.	☐	☐
7 Single parents		
a live with their family.	☐	☐
b often go out to work.	☐	☐
c never go out to work.	☐	☐
8 Old relatives		
a stay with the family.	☐	☐
b go to a home.	☐	☐
c go to a hospital.	☐	☐

Did Ida mention any of the ideas you wrote down in Activity 2? Are you surprised by any of her answers?

4

Are customs the same in Norway? Work in groups and write down your ideas.

Listen to Jan talking and tick a, b or c in the boxes under Jan. Are you surprised by any of his answers?

5

What do you think about what Ida and Jan say? Discuss in pairs.

6

You are going to interview somebody about their family. First prepare some questions. Use the interviews in this unit to help you.

Then interview another student and make notes about their answers.

- *How many brothers and sisters have you got?*
-
-
-
-
-

Homework

Write a short article describing the interview for your local newspaper.

Language Summary

Adverbs of frequency

The father **usually** goes out to work.
Marriage between people from different cultures is **always** difficult.
Men **don't usually** spend enough time with their children.

see practice page 80

Lesson 1 *Murder at Château Firenze*

Language focus: Past continuous and past simple

Skills focus: Reading and listening for specific information
Speaking: speculating

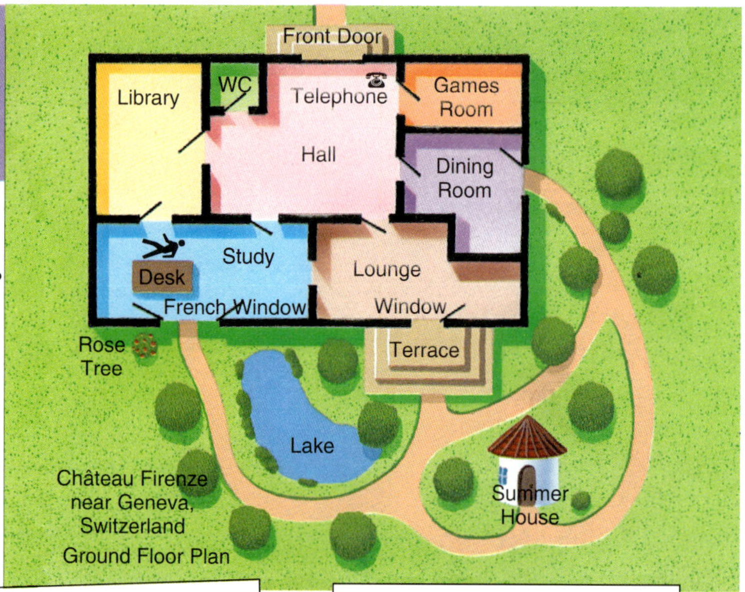

1

Work in pairs. What famous detectives do you know of? eg Sherlock Holmes. What do you know about them?

2

This is a story about a murder which took place at the Château Firenze in Switzerland in 1926. Read about the characters in the story and the summary of what happened. What do you think are the most important clues to the murder?

What happened

The murder happened at the Château Firenze near Geneva, Switzerland, the home of Sir Dennis and Lady Francesca. Three shots were heard at about 11.30 pm. The body of Sir Dennis was found in the study. Someone had shot him three times in the back. A piece of green material was found on the rose tree next to the French window. There was an unfinished letter to the Contessa on the desk. The next day a gun was found in the lake.

Sir Dennis Greyson (the dead man)

63, British businessman and art collector. His hobby was flying aeroplanes. He had business problems and borrowed a lot of money from Swiss banks. His art collection contained some very valuable Spanish paintings.

Lady Francesca Greyson

47, British wife of Sir Dennis. She inherited the Château from her parents, who were both killed in a flying accident. She was very worried about Sir Dennis' money problems and debts to the bank. She recently spoke to her lawyer about selling the Château.

Max de Selles

40, French art dealer and old family friend. Sir Dennis recently bought several paintings from him. Max's father, also a famous art dealer, and Sir Dennis were close friends for many years until he sold Sir Dennis a fake painting. The two men never spoke to each other again.

Agnes Johansson

36, Swedish fashion designer. As a young girl, she lived in Africa with her parents where she learnt how to use a gun. She met Lady Francesca at a fashion show in Paris. Lady Francesca liked her clothes and she and Agnes became close friends.

Contessa Gabriella Espinosa

31, Spanish artist. The Contessa never knew her father, who died when she was a baby. At school, she was a very good athlete. She later studied art in Paris. Sir Dennis was very kind to her.

3

Max de Selles telephoned the police, who arrived at the Château at midnight and interviewed everyone in the house. Read the first part of each person's interview, and make notes about where each person was and what they were doing.

Lady Francesca

From about 10 o'clock I was in the library. I was reading when I heard three shots. It was about 11.30. I immediately ran into the study. I found my husband dead on the floor. The French windows were open so I went outside, but there was nobody there. I came back into the study and saw Max de Selles and we then went into the hall to telephone the police. Then I think Agnes Johansson came into the hall from the lounge.

Max de Selles

I was in the games room. I was playing cards alone when I heard some shots. I immediately went across the hall into the study. I found Sir Dennis lying on the floor. There wasn't anybody else in the room. I was still looking at the body in horror when Lady Francesca came in through the French windows.

Agnes Johansson

After dinner I took a book from the library and a glass of whisky and went out onto the terrace. I was reading on the terrace when I saw somebody in the summer-house. Then someone ran along the path near the lake and went into the study. I didn't hear any shots. I went into the hall when I heard someone call.

The Contessa

I was walking in the garden. I left the dining room and went along the path to the summer-house. Then I walked back across the terrace to the Château. I didn't see anybody. When I entered the house everybody was standing in the hall. They told me Sir Dennis was dead.

Homework

Sherlock Holmes wrote a letter to his friend, Doctor Watson, about the murder at the Château. Write the letter. Say who the murderer was and why they killed Sir Dennis.

4

Look at the interviews again and draw the movements of Lady Francesca, the Contessa, Agnes Johansson and Max de Selles on the plan of the Château.

5

Now listen to the second part of each interview and make notes.

6

Work in pairs. Who do you think murdered Sir Dennis? Why? Join with another pair and discuss your ideas.

Example

I think Agnes Johansson murdered Sir Dennis because she didn't like him. And she was wearing green.

But so was Lady Francesca. I don't think that's a very good reason. I think …

Language Summary

Past continuous and past simple

Sir Dennis **was** in the study. He **was lying** on the floor.

I **was reading** when I **heard** three shots.

anybody, nobody, somebody, everybody

There wasn't **anybody** else in the room.

I saw **somebody** in the summer-house.

see practice page 81

Lesson 2 *Time capsules*

Language focus: Past simple passive

Skills focus: Reading and listening for specific information

1

What is this building? Where is it? When was it built?

2

How much do you know about the Egyptian Pyramids? Look at these statements. Are they true or false?

1 The Pyramids were built thousands of years ago. ___

2 We know how the Great Pyramid was built. ___

3 The tombs contained everything the pharaoh would need for the next life. ___

4 The pyramids had many passages to protect the pharaoh from robbers. ___

5 Pharaohs' bodies were found inside the tombs. ___

Work in pairs and compare your answers.

Now read the text and check your predictions.

The Pyramids are the oldest of the Seven Wonders of the World, but even today, in the age of advanced technology, they seem a great achievement. Forty important pyramids were built along the Nile, but the Great Pyramid of Cheops is the biggest. It is the largest single building in the world, and was completed in 1690 BC. It is said that it took 100,000 workers 22 years to complete, and 2,300,000 blocks of stone were used.

Archaeologists are not totally sure how the Great Pyramid was built. They know that a site was chosen on the west bank of the Nile, and was then made flat. The site looked north towards the Polar Star. Stone was cut from a quarry and made into the correct shape. Next the blocks of stone were put into place. The blocks were so heavy (some weighed over 2 tonnes) that some people believe they were transported by boat when the river flooded. We are still not certain how the final stones were put into position.

The Egyptians believed in an 'after-life', so everything the pharaoh needed for the 'after-life' was placed inside the pyramid: household goods, clothes, treasure – even food and drink. His servants were also buried with him. The Egyptians believed that to go into the 'after-life' the body of the pharaoh must not be disturbed, so a system of passages and tunnels was built in the Pyramids to confuse robbers. One unsolved mystery about the Pyramids is that no bodies were ever discovered in them.

3

Find the words below in the text and match them with their definitions.

1 BC	**a** a place where people are buried
2 a pharaoh	**b** the side of a river
3 a quarry	**c** a time before Christ
4 a tomb	**d** an Egyptian king
5 a bank	**e** a person who studies ancient remains
6 an archaeologist	**f** a place where stone comes from

4

Archaeologists today do not know everything about the pyramids. Look at the text again and underline three things they are not sure about.

5

Complete the following sentences using the information in the text.

1 In 1690 BC
the Great Pyramid of Cheops was completed.

2 2,300,000 blocks of stone
____

3 After a site for the Great Pyramid was chosen
____

4 Some people think that the blocks
____

5 Household goods, clothes, treasure, food and drink
____

6 The pharaohs' bodies
____

6

Work in pairs. Look at the picture. What are the people doing?

Now read this definition of a time capsule.

> time capsule (*n*) – a container filled with objects which illustrate life today. It is buried or hidden so that when people open it in the future, they will know what life is like now.

How is a time capsule similar to a pyramid?

Homework

Imagine your time capsule is discovered at the end of the 21st century. Write a short article for your local newspaper. Use the text in Activity 7 to help you.

7

Listen to part of a local radio report about a time capsule and answer these questions.

- Where was the capsule buried?
- What was in it?
- Who attended the ceremony?
- What did builders find in the school?

Complete the gaps in the text with the correct form of the verbs in the box.

attend bury discover find hide open put

Time seemed to stand still at Hollingworth Primary School yesterday when a time capsule (1) *was buried* in the school grounds. The time capsule (2) __________ at a special ceremony at the village school which (3) __________ by pupils, teachers and parents. Modern coins, photographs of all the children, a copy of the local newspaper and some information about the school and the village (4) __________ inside a special box. An old time capsule from 1860 (5) __________ at the school by builders, but when it (6) __________, the contents (7) __________ to be damaged. It contained a broken wine bottle, some Victorian money and a newspaper which was too wet to read.

Listen to the report again and check your answers.

8

Write down five things you would put in a time capsule. Work in groups and compare your lists. Decide on five things for your group's time capsule. They should represent this year and your country.

Language Summary

Past simple passive
The Pyramids **were built** thousands of years ago.
Archaeologists are not totally sure how the Great Pyramid **was built**.

Determiners: *some, a, an*
It contained **a** broken wine bottle, **some** Victorian money and **a** newspaper.

see practice page 82

Lesson 3 *The Olympic Games*

Language focus: Direct and indirect *Wh-* questions
Skills focus: Reading and listening for specific information
Writing questions

1

What do you know about the Olympic Games? What would you like to know? Work in pairs and write five questions that you would like to know the answers to.

Example *When did the Olympic Games start?*

Read the text and see if it answers any of your questions.

The Olympic Games have changed greatly since the first contest in Olympia, western Greece, in 776 BC. The first Olympic Games lasted for one day and had only one event – a running race the length of the stadium – and only men competed. Nowadays the Olympic Games have several hundred events for both men and women and last for over two weeks. The Games are a multi-million dollar extravaganza, and many people feel that they are now more concerned with money, politics and entertainment than with athletic competition.

The ancient games in Olympia ended when the Romans conquered Greece, and none were held for 1500 years. However, when the ruins of the stadium of Olympia were discovered in 1875, a Frenchman, Baron de Coubertin, had the idea of organising a modern, international Olympics. These were first held in Athens in 1896 and are now held in a different country every four years. The modern Olympic Games consist of a Summer and a Winter Games. Baron de Coubertin was also responsible for the Olympic symbol of the five rings, which are black, blue, green, red and yellow, and represent the five continents.

The ancient Olympics were held in honour of Zeus, the supreme Greek God. The Olympic flame, which is lit at the opening ceremony, traditionally comes from the Gods. Thousands of runners carry the flame from the valley of Olympia to the stadium. This journey starts four weeks before the opening of the games and the runners represent each country which lies between Greece and the country holding the games. For the 1992 Olympics in Barcelona Antonio Rebollo lit the flame in the Olympic stadium with an arrow. He had trained for eight months and fired 2,000 practice shots for his big moment which lasted two seconds!

2

Write questions for these answers.

1 *When did the Olympic Games start?* ______ In 776 BC.
2 ______ Two weeks.
3 ______ When the Romans conquered Greece.
4 ______ Baron de Coubertin.
5 ______ Five interlocking rings.
6 ______ Black, blue, green, red and yellow.
7 ______ From the Gods.
8 ______ In Barcelona.

3

Work in pairs. Look at the text again. Write down as many differences between the ancient and the modern Olympics as you can find.

Example

Ancient Olympics – Athletic competition important
Modern Olympics – Money, politics, entertainment more important

4

Answer the questions in this Olympic quiz.

1 What does the word 'Olympiad' mean? Is it:
- **a** a period of four years between the games? ☐
- **b** an Ancient Greek sport? ☐
- **c** a type of medal? ☐

2 Does the host country always come first in the procession at the opening ceremony?
Yes/No

3 How many countries do the athletes represent?
- **a** 90 ☐
- **b** 120 ☐
- **c** more than 140 ☐

4 Where did Carl Lewis win four Olympic gold medals?
- **a** Barcelona ☐
- **b** Seoul ☐
- **c** Los Angeles ☐

5 Are the Olympic gold medals solid gold?
Yes/No

6 Which five sports make up the modern pentathlon?

canoeing ☐ fencing ☐ gymnastics ☐ horse riding ☐

long jump ☐ pistol shooting ☐ running ☐ swimming ☐

7 Does the UN choose the host city for the Olympics?
Yes/No

8 When did Moscow host the Olympic Games?
- **a** 1980 ☐
- **b** 1984 ☐
- **c** 1988 ☐

9 No Olympic Games were held in 1914, 1940 and 1944. Why not?

____

Compare your answers with another student.

5

Now listen to William doing the quiz on a radio show. Make a note of William's answers.

6

Finally listen to the correct answers to the quiz and make a note of them. How many answers did William get right? How many answers did you get right? Compare your results with other students.

7

Work in groups. Write six questions for a sports quiz. Then join another group. Ask them your questions and answer theirs.

Homework

Write a quiz of six questions or more on a different topic to ask other students in your class.

Language Summary

Direct *Wh-* questions
What does the word 'Olympiad' mean?

Indirect *Wh-* questions
Do you know what the word 'Olympiad' means?

see practice page 83

Lesson 1 *An unusual collection*

Language focus: Present perfect and past simple

Skills focus: Speaking: talking about collections and travel experiences
Listening for specific information

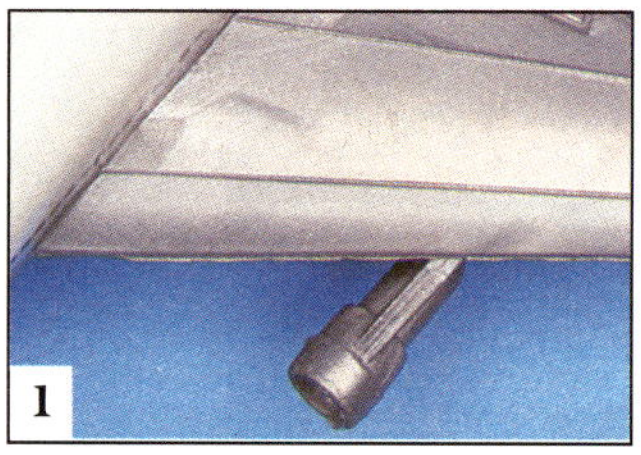
1

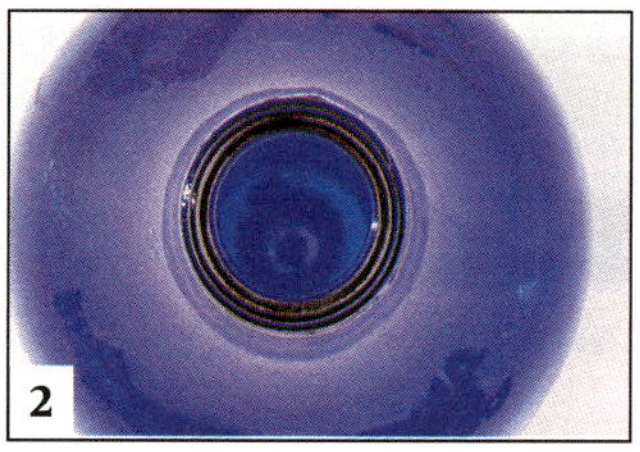
2

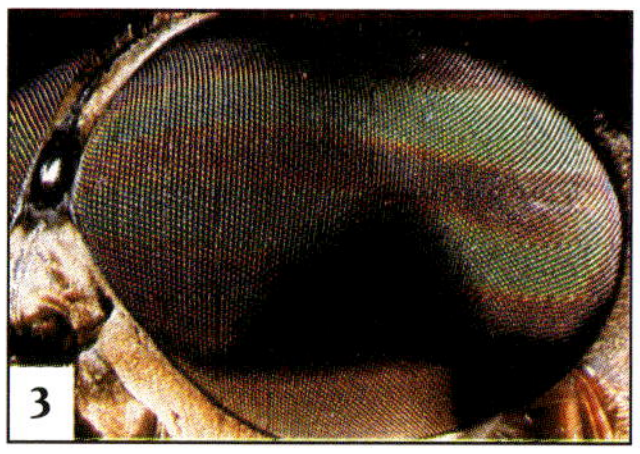
3

4

1

Look at the photographs of some things that people collect. What do you think they are?

Would you like to collect any of these things?

You have been given a lot of money to start a collection. What three things would you collect and why? Discuss with a partner.

2

Match the airline logos with their countries.

Australia *4*

Japan ___

The Netherlands ___

Spain ___

Venezuela ___

1 JAL

2 VIASA

3 KLM

4 QANTAS

5 IBERIA

3

You are going to listen to an interview with Sandra who collects things from planes. Match the items in the picture with the words in the box.

e.g. menu *a*

comb knife luggage label ~~menu~~
pilot's hat poster scarf shoe horn spoon
sugar toothbrush toothpaste

Which items do you think Sandra has in her collection?

Now listen and tick the items Sandra has.

4

Listen again. Which of the statements are true? Which are false?

1 She's collected over a hundred items. T
2 She can see the airport from her flat. ___
3 She likes flying. ___
4 She started her collection five years ago. ___
5 Her favourite object in the collection is a poster. ___
6 She got a Lufthansa scarf from a friend. ___
7 Her collection is in her living room. ___
8 She has got a spoon from Egypt Air. ___

What would Sandra now like for her collection? Is she likely to get it?

5

Why do you think Sandra gets frightened when she is flying? Discuss with a partner.

Now read part of a magazine article about her and check your predictions.

Sandra became frightened of flying on one of her first flights when she took a small plane to the south of Ecuador. First there was a lot of turbulence, which made her feel sick. Then, when they were near the airport, the pilot made an announcement:

'Unfortunately our landing will be delayed as we have not received permission to land yet .'

The plane circled the airport for over an hour. Sandra felt sure they would run out of fuel. Eventually the pilot tried to land the plane, but, as they were coming down onto the runway, the plane suddenly rose back into the sky. The pilot made another announcement:

'We apologise, but we have just received new landing instructions.'

By this time Sandra and all the other passengers were very nervous. They held their breath as the pilot made a second attempt to land the plane. They hit the ground so hard that some of the oxygen masks fell down. Sandra screamed. The plane bumped dangerously along the runway, and finally stopped just before the grass at the end.

'We have just landed at Loja airport,' the pilot announced happily. 'We hope you have enjoyed your flight.'

6

Now complete the sentences about the text.

1 Sandra felt sick because
____
2 Because the pilot didn't have landing permission, they
____
3 After circling the airport for an hour, the pilot
____
4 Some of the oxygen masks came down because
____
5 When the plane landed, Sandra
____

7

Work in groups. How do you feel about travelling in planes, buses, boats, etc? Have you ever had any bad experiences? Tell your group about them.

Homework

Write a letter to a friend telling them about one of your travel experiences.

Language Summary

Present perfect and past simple
She**'s collected** over 100 items.
She **started** her collection five years ago.

already, yet and *just*
I've **already** collected over 100 things.
We have not received permission to land **yet**.
We have **just** landed at Loja airport.

see practice page 84

Lesson 2 *Collecting information*

Language focus: Present perfect simple and present perfect continuous

Skills focus: Listening for main ideas
Writing: conducting a survey and writing up notes

1

What are these people doing? What do you think they are talking about?

Have you ever been interviewed about anything? If so, what were you interviewed about?

2

Listen to four interviews. Which of the topics in the box are the people talking about? Write down the topics in the order that you hear them talked about.

airline services education hobbies music shopping sport television travel work

	topic	key words
1	*education*	*school, subjects, study, History, English*
2		
3		
4		

Listen again and write down the key words that helped you identify the topic. Compare your answers with a partner.

3

Read the notes the interviewer made on Jacob Westbrook's hobby of collecting bottles. Then complete her report using the notes.

NAME Jacob Westbrook
AGE 22
ADDRESS 201 Edge Lane, Liverpool, Merseyside
JOB Engineering student
MAIN LEISURE INTEREST
WHERE/WHEN?

Collecting bottles

WHY?

Weekends in antique shops/auctions

ADDITIONAL INFORMATION

Started when he got a ship in a bottle as a birthday present from his uncle

300 bottles in collection

Been collecting 10 years

Collection contains - ships in bottles, miniatures (brandy, rum, etc) & unusual shaped bottles

Best item - a bottle in bluish glass in the shape of a fish

Last week I interviewed (1) *Jacob Westbrook* who is a (2) ________ -year-old (3) *engineering student* from Liverpool. His hobby is (4) ________.

It's a hobby he started (5) ________ he was only twelve. It began when his uncle (6) ________.

Since then his collection has grown and he has now got (7) ________. His favourite bottle is (8) ________.

4

Work in groups. Choose a topic for a survey eg holidays, sports, films, music, books, TV. Write eight questions to ask some other students. Start the questions with:

1 Have you ever ...?

2 What ...?

3 When ...?

4 How ...?

5

Interview four other students each and note down their answers. Compare your results with your group and report your findings to the class.

Homework

Write up the results of one of your interviews.

Example

I interviewed ... about ...
He/She ...

Language Summary

Present perfect simple and present perfect continuous

How much TV **have** you **watched** this week?
I**'ve been watching** more than usual this week.

Polite requests

Could you spare a couple of minutes, please?
May I just ask a few questions?
Would you mind answering a few questions?

see practice page 85

Lesson 3 *'The Collector'*

Language focus: *-ing* form

Skills focus: Reading a narrative
Speaking: roleplaying a police interview

1

Look at the picture. What is the man doing? What do you think he is like?

2

You are going to read a short extract from 'The Collector' by John Fowles. The story is about a lonely man called Frederick who takes photographs and collects butterflies. One day he wins a lot of money and buys a large house in the country. He plans to catch a butterfly he has been watching for two years – a young woman called Miranda.

Work in groups. How do you think Frederick will try to catch Miranda? Will he succeed?

Now read the extract and check your predictions. Ignore the gaps.

Who is telling the story?

Why do you think Frederick has kidnapped Miranda?

What do you think will happen to Miranda and Frederick?

She came out alone, exactly two hours later, it had stopped raining more or less and it was almost dark, the sky was overcast. I watched her go back the usual way up the hill. Then I drove off past her to a place where I knew she must (1) __________.

There was just this one place.

Two old women with (2) __________ (it began to spot with rain again) appeared and came up the road towards me. It was just what I didn't want, I knew she was due, and I nearly gave up then and there. But I bent right down, they passed talking nineteen to the dozen, I don't think they even saw me or the van. There were cars parked everywhere in that district. A minute passed. I got out and opened the back. It was all planned. And then she was near. She'd come up and round without me seeing, only twenty yards away, walking quickly. I could see there was (3) __________ behind her.

Then she was right beside me, coming up the pavement. Funny, singing to herself.

I said, 'Excuse me, do you know anything about dogs?'

She stopped, (4) __________. 'Why?' she said.

'It's (5) __________. I've just run one over,' I said. 'It dashed out. I don't know what to do with it. It's not dead. I looked into the back very worried.'

'Oh, poor thing,' she said.

She came towards me, to look in. Just as I hoped.

'There's no blood,' I said, 'but it can't (6) __________.'

Then she came round the end of the open back door, and I stood back as if to let her see. She bent forward to peer in, I flashed a look down the road, no one, and then I got her.

3

Work in pairs. Choose the most appropriate word to fill in the gaps in the text. Check your answers in pairs.

1 live	pass	visit
2 umbrellas	glasses	newspapers
3 a friend	no one	a police officer
4 frightened	surprised	angry
5 awful	great	interesting
6 sleep	eat	move

4

Listen to the radio report about Miranda's disappearance and fill in the police report form.

MISSING PERSON REPORT FORM

Name: *Miranda* ____________

Age: ____________

Address: *Hampstead* ____________

____

____

Occupation: ____________

Description:

Height: *5'4'* ____________

Build: ____________

Hair: *long* ____________

Clothes: *blue* ____________

Place of disappearance:

between the cinema and ____________

Time: *between* ____________

Homework

Write up the police report from Activity 5.

5

Work in pairs. Student A – you are the police officer. Student B – you are a witness who saw Miranda that afternoon. Roleplay the interview.

Use the information in the extract in Activity 2, the missing person report form in Activity 4 and your imagination.

Then change roles.

Student A

Ask questions such as:

- When did you see Miranda?
- What was she doing?
- What were you doing?
- What was she wearing?
- Did you see anything suspicious?

Student B

Answer the police officer's questions.

Language Summary

-ing form

Then she was right beside me, **coming** up the pavement.

They passed **talking** nineteen to the dozen.

see practice page 86

Unit 8 A week of entertainment

Lesson 1 *What's on?*

Language focus: Making and replying to suggestions

Skills focus: Reading a programme for specific information
Speaking: making arrangements

1

2

3

1

Work in pairs. Look at the photographs. What are the people doing and which countries do you think the activities come from?

Have you tried to do any of the activities? Would you like to?

2

Look at the programme for this international festival and tick the events that are advertised.

- ☑ a bagpiper
- ☐ a dinner
- ☐ an exhibition
- ☐ a fashion show
- ☐ fireworks
- ☐ a marathon
- ☐ mime
- ☐ a play
- ☐ a talk

Wenton International Festival

Sunday
International Dinner
Traditional food from all over the world! While you eat there'll be music from many different countries, and there'll be traditional folk dancing after dinner.

8pm – County Hall
adults £7 children £3

Monday
Batik
Come and try this ancient Indonesian art form. Bring your own cotton or silk and learn how to create your own designs.

Monday, Wednesday & Friday 6-8pm – City Hall
£10 for all three sessions

Scottish Dancing
A lively, entertaining evening! Come and hear Iain Macdonald playing the bagpipes and learn some traditional Scottish dances. Fun for everyone!

8pm – County Hall
FREE

Tuesday
Tai Chi
What's it all about? Expert Xu Chang will be giving a short talk on the philosophy and origins of what is often called 'meditation in movement'. Then you too can learn some of the basic movements. Wear casual clothes.

7.30pm – Sports Centre
£5

Ballet Classique
The well-known French dance company performs the beautiful and moving Swan Lake by Tchaikovsky. Don't miss it!

7.30pm – City Theatre
adults £10 children £5

Wednesday
Film Day
2.30pm – Aladdin – The Walt Disney classic for children.

7.30pm – Cinema Paradiso – The award winning Italian film about a young boy's dreams of becoming a film director.

10pm – Lethal Weapon – Mel Gibson in this exciting action thriller.

City Theatre
adults £3.50 children £2.50

Thursday
Russian Acrobats
An unforgettable experience with a Moscow company: balancing acts, fire-eating, flying across the floor and in the air – you'll be amazed!

7.30pm – City Theatre
adults £6 children £3

Friday
Ted Edwards – The Camel Man
Ted's slide show and talk about his amazing experiences during his solo crossing of the south-western Sahara.

8.00pm – County Hall
£2

Saturday
Festival Fun Run
This is not a marathon, half-marathon or even a mini-marathon – it's just a gentle jog for all the family.

2.30pm – Sports Centre
FREE

Firework Display
Hot soup and baked potatoes to keep you warm while you watch the spectacular firework display.

8.00pm – South Park
FREE

The Samba Sensation
Finish the festival by dancing to the tropical sound of one of the best Samba groups from Rio. Feel the heat! Cocktail bar.

9.00pm – City Hall
£5

3

Listen to three friends talking about the festival. Which events do they agree to go to together?

4

Which phrases do Suzie, Brian and Geoff use to make, accept and reject suggestions? Listen to parts of their conversation again and fill in the gaps.

1 Suzie: Well it starts with a dinner and folk dancing on Sunday. *How about going to dinner?*
Geoff: __________ .

2 Geoff: And __________ to a club or something afterwards.
Suzie: I __________ Scottish dancing. It's on the programme for Monday. __________ that?
Brian: Yeah, __________. It would be good for a laugh.
Geoff: I'm __________. I'm playing chess on Monday.

3 Geoff: And ... er ... __________ cinema one night?
Suzie: Well, I __________ something different – we can see a film anytime.
Geoff: OK. Well, __________ the Moscow acrobats?

5

Read the programme again and tick five events you would like to go to.

Work in groups. Agree on five events you are going to go to together. Use phrases from Activity 4 to help you make suggestions.

Fill in your diary for the week. Write down the events, times and places.

How much money are you going to spend in total?

11 Monday __________

12 Tuesday __________

13 Wednesday __________

14 Thursday __________

15 Friday __________

16 Saturday __________

17 Sunday __________

Homework

Write a short newspaper report on one of the events you went to see at the festival.

6

Read these newspaper reports on two of the festival events. Which events are they? Did the writer enjoy them? Underline the words that helped you decide.

1 Last night was my first experience of __________. The acts were performed with incredible energy and skill. Some of them were extremely dangerous. However, it was a very entertaining event and the audience clearly enjoyed themselves.

2 Where was the fun, our reporter asks. Many families came to participate in the festival __________ but the cold weather, and the awful organisation made people go home early. What's more, the course was too long for many of the young children. A disappointing event!

Language Summary

Making and replying to suggestions

What about going Scottish dancing?
I'm sorry, I can't.
How about some spaghetti? **OK, fine.**
Why don't we watch the fireworks?
Let's go to a club.
Shall we go to the cinema?

Stating preferences

I'd prefer to go Scottish dancing.

see practice page 87

Lesson 2 *A celebrity guest*

Language focus: Non-defining relative clauses

Skills focus: Listening to a talk for main ideas and details
Writing a publicity article

1

Ted Edwards was a celebrity guest who was invited to this year's international festival to talk about his journey across the Sahara Desert. All the numbers in the box are important to his story. What do you think they refer to?

45° nineteen-day 25 kilograms
two 1983 350

Now read an article about Ted that appeared in the festival brochure. Complete the article using the numbers in the box.

Ted Edwards – The Camel Man

IN FEBRUARY (1) __________, Ted Edwards, who was once a school drama teacher, and who is a keen folk-singer and adventurer, completed a (2) __________ journey, which involved travelling (3) __________ miles across the Sahara: the longest self-sufficient solo journey in history.

First he went to Timbuktu, where he bought (4) __________ camels. Then he set out on his epic journey, but he soon ran into problems. He was stung by a scorpion, he fell off a camel and broke several bones, he got lost and ran out of water in temperatures of over (5) __________ and he suffered from the hot sun, wind and sand. Eventually, after almost three weeks, he reached his destination, where the BBC television crew, who were waiting for him, had given up hope of seeing him alive. He weighed (6) __________ less than when he had set off.

2

Look at the article again and answer these questions.

What was Ted's job?
Why was his journey important?
How did he break some bones?
Who met him at the end of the journey?

3

Ted was invited to another festival to talk about another adventure he had. Work in pairs and look at the pictures. Where do you think Ted went? What did he see there?

Listen to the start of Ted's talk and number the pictures in the order he talks about them.

4

Listen again and make notes to complete the table.

Where Ted went	
When he went	
Length of journey	
What he did	*climbed on a glacier,*
Who he met	
Problems he had	*fell climbing the glacier,*

Compare your table with your partner.

Which of Ted's journeys do you think was:
- more interesting? Why?
- more dangerous? Why?

Would you like to do a similar journey? Why/Why not?

Homework

Write the article for the festival brochure. Use the article in Activity 1 to help you.

5

Work in pairs. You are going to write an article for a festival brochure about Ted Edwards' talk. Think of a title and choose a picture from Activity 3 to illustrate it. Look at the notes you made in Activity 4 and decide what information to include.

Language Summary

Non-defining relative clauses

This is me on the top of Mount Hekla, **which** last erupted in 1981.

Ted Edwards, **who** was once a school drama teacher ...

First he went to Timbuktu, **where** he bought two camels.

Phrasal verbs

Then he **set out on** his epic journey, but he soon **ran into** problems.

see practice page 88

Lesson 3 *Choosing a programme*

Language focus: Talking about likes and dislikes
Expressing agreement and disagreement

Skills focus: Speaking: roleplaying a committee meeting
Writing: making a festival programme

1

Work in groups. What items can you see in the picture? What possible festival activities do they suggest?

Example

microphone – pop concert/karaoke/song contest/a comedian

Can you think of any other possible activities for a festival?

2

Look at the suggestions for the next festival and tick four events in the table that you would like to include. Explain your choices to another student.

Now listen to the committee discussing the next festival and fill in the second column. Put a tick (✓) next to the events they agree on, a cross (✗) next to the events they disagree on or a question mark (?) next to the events they don't make a decision on.

Did the committee choose any of the events you chose?

3

Listen again and make notes on the reasons they give for their decisions in the third column.

Do you think they give good reasons?

	Your choice	The committee's choice	Reasons
a pop group		✗	*too expensive, town hall too small*
a jazz group		✓	popular
5-a-side football		X	interested, no decent pitch
Greek folk group		✓	different, spectacular
children's art exhibition		✓	parents will like it
lecture/slide show on Everest		?	
fancy-dress disco		X	difficult to sell costumes
celebrity golf match		?	

4

You are on the festival committee for your town or city. You are going to plan a one-week festival.

Here are some useful phrases from Activity 2.

a Starting a meeting: *Are we ready to start the meeting?*
b Interrupting: *Sorry, could I just say something here?*
c Continuing: *Could I just finish?*
d Changing the subject: *Let's move on to ...*
e Finishing the meeting: *I think that's all we need to discuss.*

Which phrases below have a similar function to the ones above from the committee meeting?

1 Now the next item on the agenda is ... *d*

2 I'd just like to say one more thing. ______

3 That's all we have time for. ______

4 Let's begin with ... ______

5 May I interrupt? ______

5

Now plan your festival programme in groups of four.

Student A – you are the chairperson of the committee.
Student B – you are the director of music and dance.
Student C – you are the director of films and theatre.
Student D – you are the director of sports and leisure activities.

Read your rolecard and have a committee meeting to discuss the events you are going to include.

Note the following:
- the festival lasts a week
- you need a good mixture of events
- you need at least two events each day
- you need to decide prices, times and venues.

Student A Chairperson of the committee

You are in charge of the meeting.

You want a good mixture of events, but you don't like the idea of a pop concert because the police always complain about the noise.

You want to charge an entrance fee to all events because last year the festival lost money.

Homework

Complete your part of the festival brochure for your classroom display.

Student B Director of music and dance

You want to invite a famous pop group this year. You know this will be a success because a lot of people suggested inviting a pop goup last year. You think it should be on the last night.

You think that there were too many films last year.

You would like half-price tickets for children.

Student C Director of films and theatre

You want a film every night because you know people enjoy watching good films.

You want evening events to start at 8pm to give people time to have dinner first.

You want to invite a famous theatre group to the festival but they are very expensive, so you want them to perform for three nights.

Student D Director of sports/leisure activities

You want special activities for children every day.

You think evening events should start early so that more children can go to them.

You want a big event on the last night for the whole town.

You would like half-price tickets for children.

6

Now write your festival programme. Divide the work between the group. You need a programme of events and articles about your celebrity guests.

Use the programme in Lesson 1 and the article in Lesson 2 to help you.

Language Summary

Talking about likes and dislikes
You know people **enjoy watching** good films.
You **don't like** the idea of a pop group.

Expressing agreement and disagreement
I think it's too difficult to get costumes. – **So do I.**
I don't think this is a good idea. – **Neither do I.**
I don't think the town hall's too small. – **Well, I do.**

see practice page 89

Unit 9 The natural world

Lesson 1 *Whales*

Language focus: Comparatives with *as* ... *as*; revision of comparatives and superlatives

Skills focus: Reading a factual text for main idea and detail
Listening to a radio discussion and expressing opinions

1

Write down three things you know about whales.

Compare your list with two other students.

2

Look at the photo and match the items with the words below.

Tick the items which you think could have parts made from whales.

- ☐ **1** candle ___c___
- ☐ **2** detergent ______
- ☐ **3** face cream ______
- ☐ **4** lipstick ______
- ☐ **5** margarine ______
- ☐ **6** medicine ______
- ☐ **7** paint ______
- ☐ **8** perfume ______
- ☐ **9** tennis racket ______
- ☐ **10** umbrella ______

Compare your answers with another student.

Check your answers with your teacher.

3

Work in pairs. Look at these statements. Do you think they are true or false? Discuss with your partner.

1 Whales have existed for 70 million years. _F_

2 They are not as developed as humans. ___

3 The Blue Whale is 60 metres long. ___

4 The Blue Whale is not as large as a dinosaur. ___

5 Whales can stay underwater for two hours without breathing. ___

6 Whales can navigate by sound. ___

7 Whales sometimes don't eat for months. ___

Now read the text and check your predictions.

1 'Whales' is a general term which includes dolphins and porpoises. They have existed for over 70,000 years, and, after humans, they are nature's most developed creatures.

2 The Blue Whale can measure over 30 metres in length and weigh as much as 150 tonnes – the equivalent of 200 cars. It is the largest creature that has ever lived. It has seven stomachs, consumes a million calories a day and can live for 120 years.

3 Whales are remarkable creatures. They can stay underwater for up to an hour without breathing. They also have the most sophisticated sound and communication system of any animal. Whales whistle and sing to each other. They also use sound signals for navigation. The Blue Whale's whistle, which has been measured at 188 decibels, is louder than Concorde.

4 Whales can survive for as long as eight months without eating and some travel as far as 5,000 kilometres each way from where they feed to where they breed. They feed on fish, seafood, and plankton, but, unlike most animals, they spend much more time playing than looking for food. They are gentle creatures that help each other, and there have also been cases when whales have helped humans at sea.

Which fact most suprised you?

4

In which paragraphs are these topics mentioned?

the Blue Whale ___*2*___

breathing ______

communication ______

feeding habits ______

length of time in existence ______

navigation ______

playing ______

types of whales ______

Homework

Complete this letter to the radio station expressing your opinion on whaling.

Dear Sir/Madam,
After listening to the radio phone-in on whales, I must say I agree with ... because I think ... .
I also think ...

Finish your letter with *Yours faithfully* and sign your name.

5

What is this picture about? What do you feel about it?

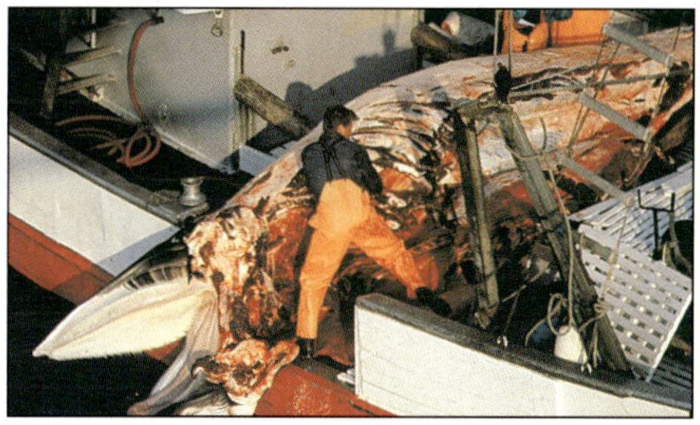

6

Listen to part of a radio phone-in about whaling. Which person supports whaling, and which person is against it?

Listen again and mark the reasons each person gives for their opinion. Mark A next to the reasons given by Ms Darracott, and B next to those given by Mr Strowbridge.

1 Whaling provides jobs. *A*

2 Whales can be dangerous. ___

3 Some types of whale are close to extinction. ___

4 Whales are beautiful. ___

5 Whaling is part of a cultural tradition. ___

6 Humans are more important than whales. ___

7 Whales help control the environment. ___

8 Whales are an important source of meat. ___

9 Whales are important for medicine. ___

10 Humans can learn a lot from whales. ___

Tick three points you agree with. Find another student who has the opposite opinions and explain your opinions to them.

Language Summary

Comparatives with *as ... as*
The Blue Whale can weigh **as** much **as** 150 tonnes.
The situation is**n't as** bad **as** that.

Revision of comparatives and superlatives
The Blue Whale's whistle ... is **louder than** Concorde.
It is **the largest** creature that has ever lived.

Revision of the present perfect
They **have existed** for over 70,000 years.

see practice page 90

Lesson 2 *Favourite animals*

Language focus: Reported speech

Skills focus: Listening to and writing descriptions of animals
Reading a newspaper article

1

Work in groups. Which animals do you associate with the following subjects? You have five minutes to write down as many as you can think of.

cartoons clothes science sport

Example

cartoons: mouse, rabbit, ...
clothes: fox, ...
science: rat, ...
sport: horse, ...

Compare your list with another group.

2

What are the animals in the picture? What do you think the newspaper article is about? Read the article quickly and check your predictions.

Police tracking smells from the small Frankfurt flat of an American military historian found a crocodile in the bath, a python in the hall, and a huge arsenal of weapons.

A police visit uncovered 50 weapons, including automatic rifles, and a two metre-long crocodile swimming in the bath-tub.

Police investigator Karl-Heinz Reinstaedt told reporters that there was a python 'as thick as a thigh' in the hall. He also said that there was a lizard, almost a metre long, staring out at police from a glass cabinet.

Police said the tenant was a civilian, aged 36, who was working on a history of the third US tank division. They said that they thought he was currently on holiday in the United States. Police told reporters that US authorities were helping to locate him and said that he may face charges of violating weapons laws as well as animal protection codes.

3

Look at the article again and match the halves of the sentences.

1 The police found a python in
2 They found a lizard in
3 They found a crocodile in
4 The flat is in
5 The person who lives in the flat is
6 He is probably on holiday in
7 Karls-Heinz Reinstaedt is

a historian.
the United States.
Germany.
the bath.
the hall.
a glass cupboard.
a police investigator.

4

Look at the pictures of these famous animals. What are they? Why are they famous? Do you know anything else about them?

1

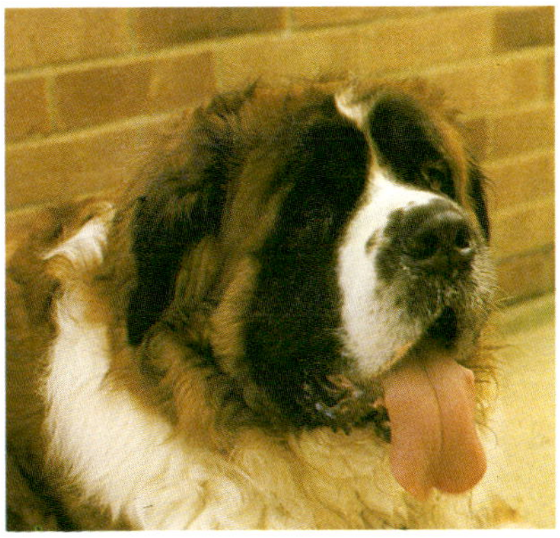

2

3

Which of the things in the box do the animals in the pictures have? Use a dictionary to help you.

beak **big ears** **feathers** **four legs** **hair** **horns** **a long tail** **a long tongue** **paws** **sharp teeth** **wings**

Example 1 – four legs, hair, ...

Homework

Write a description of an animal you are interested in. Include a physical description and any unusual facts.

5

Listen to five people describing five different animals. Write the name of each animal and the words that helped you decide in the table.

	animal	key words
1	*snake*	*long, thin, no legs, long tongue ...*
2		
3		
4		
5		

6

Work in pairs. Write a short description of an animal. Do not write the name of the animal. Swap descriptions with another pair and guess the identity of their animal.

7

Interview three other students. Find out which animals they find the most interesting and why. Work in groups and compare answers.

Example

Henri said he thought dolphins were the most interesting animals because they are so intelligent.

Which is the most popular animal?

Language Summary

Reported speech
Police **said** the tenant **was** a civilian.
Reinstaedt **told** reporters **that** there **was** a python in the hall.

say and tell
They **said** that they thought he was currently on holiday in the United States.
Police **told** reporters that US authorities were helping to locate him.

see practice page 91

Lesson 3 *Nature at work*

Language focus: Short forms

Skills focus: Reading and writing postcards
Listening for main ideas and detail

1

Look at the photographs. Where do you think the photographs were taken? Why? Have you ever experienced this type of weather?

Compare your answers with another student.

2

Listen to these sounds. What do you think is happening? Where is it happening? Which picture in Activity 1 matches the sounds?

3

The sounds in Activity 2 are from something that happened to Anthony during a holiday. Listen to Anthony's story and check the predictions you made in Activity 2.

Listen to Anthony again and answer these questions.

1 Where was Anthony?

2 Who was he with?

3 What time did they wake up?

4 Why did they wake up?

5 What happened to the hut?

6 What happened to the lights?

7 How did Anthony feel?

8 What was the beach like the next day?

4

Work in pairs. Read the three postcards. Which one did Anthony write?

Underline the words and phrases in the other two postcards that are different from Anthony's experience.

A

Dear Michel,

Holiday's great. Too hot to do anything – temperatures have been over 30°C. Had an incredible experience last night. Gloria and I were in a typhoon. Woke up at about two in the morning and could feel the hut moving. Could see palm trees falling down and huge waves. Quite frightening really, though I enjoyed the experience. Can't wait to show you my photos.

Anthony

Michel Dubois
6 rue Berthe Morisot
75006 Paris
France

B

Hi Carla !

How was your holiday? Ours is great – want to stay here for ever. We're staying in a hut on the beach. It's really hot and we've done lots of things. Last night an amazing thing happened – we were in a typhoon! Woke up in the middle of the night and were so terrified we stayed in bed. Today everything's fine again – blue sky and calm sea, but there's rubbish all over the beach. Tell you more when I get back.

Lots of love, Anthony.

Carla Morani
Via Imera 10
04023 Formia (LT)
Italy

C

Dear mum,

Having a great time. Really hot most of the time, but what an amazing experience yesterday! Gloria and I were in a typhoon. Didn't get any sleep – could hear the heavy wind and the rain, and a window broke. Lasted all day. Don't worry, we're OK. See you soon.

Love Anthony

PS Hope you're feeling better.

Mrs P Evans
21 Western Road
Swindon

5

On postcards a lot of words are missed out or shortened. For example 'Having a great time.' not 'I'm/We're having a great time.' Put a cross in all the places on these cards where there are words missing and underline the words that have been shortened. What are the missing and shortened words?

Homework

Write a postcard from your group's holiday in Activity 6. Use the postcards in Activity 4 to help you.

6

Work in groups. Invent a 'worst holiday ever' story. Each person in turn tells one part of the story using at least one word from the box.

40°C bottle dream earthquake elephant fire helicopter hospital hotel hurricane pizza police prison snow umbrella wallet

Example

We were staying in a horrible hotel next to the noisiest disco in the town.

The temperature was 40°C at night!

On the second night ...

Language Summary

Short forms

Don't worry, **we're** OK.
Having a great time.

Past continuous

We **were staying** in a horrible hotel next to the noisiest disco in the town.

see practice page 92

Lesson 1 *The Blue Nile*

Language focus: *too* and *enough*

Skills focus: Reading for main ideas and detail
Speaking: comparing information

1

Look at the photograph. Where are the people? What are they doing?

2

You are going to read about an expedition to the Blue Nile. What do you know about the River Nile?

Is it (a) 3,000 kms long?
(b) over 6,000 kms long?
(c) 5,000 kms long?

Tick the countries the river runs through:

Ethiopia Saudi Arabia Sudan Egypt South Africa

Tick the animals you can see along the banks of the Blue Nile:

tigers snakes crocodiles turtles sharks

Check your answers with your teacher.

3

Match the words with their definitions. Use a dictionary to help you.

1 a whirlpool	**a** an armed robber
2 a gorge	**b** to die under water
3 a bandit	**c** a long gun
4 a canoe	**d** a small rubber boat
5 a dinghy	**e** dangerous water that moves round in circles
6 to drown	**f** a narrow, steep-sided valley
7 to capsize	**g** a long, light boat
8 a rifle	**h** to turn over in a boat

4

Work in pairs. Student A – read story A. Student B – read story B. Put the numbers of the events on your map.

Story A

The main events

1 the first bandit attack
2 a dinghy capsized
3 Ian Macleod drowned
4 they carried the dinghies on land
5 another dinghy capsized
6 the second bandit attack

In 1968 Captain John Blashford Snell led a team of 56 down the Blue Nile. The adventure started on 8th September 1968 when three rubber dinghies left Lake Tana to go down the upper part of the Nile.

At the first waterfall one dinghy capsized. On the second day the same thing happened again and several team members nearly died. By then they had reached the Tississat Falls. There the water was too fast and dangerous for the dinghies, so they carried them on land. Once the team had passed the falls, they put the dinghies back on the river with no one in them and returned to them at the Second Portuguese Bridge. It was just before the bridge that one member, Ian Macleod, drowned trying to cross the river.

Then, one day while the team were exploring two caves, bandits attacked them with rifles and rocks. They ran for the boats and luckily escaped. That night they had just established their camp when more armed bandits arrived. Everyone escaped to the boats and started off down the river as fast as possible.

Finally on 25th September, the dinghies arrived safely at the Shafartak Bridge.

Story B

The main events

1 bandits shot at them
2 The team argument
3 Mike Jones got caught in a whirlpool
4 Glen Greer capsized
5 Steve killed a crocodile
6 the team got together again

In 1972 a twenty-year-old medical student, Mike Jones, led a five-man canoeing expedition down the upper part of the Blue Nile. The other members of the team were Mike Hopkinson, Glen Greer, Steve Nash and Dave Burkinshaw.

On 3rd September they started out and at first everything went well, but then Glen capsized. He survived, but the canoe was badly damaged. The next day at the Tissisat Falls there was a team crisis. Dave and Steve didn't think it was safe enough to continue. There was a long argument and in the end the two Mikes continued in their canoes while the other three carried their equipment on land. The team arranged to meet at the second Portuguese bridge. The water in the gorge was very fast and dangerous, but luckily both canoeists were experienced enough to get through. Just before they reached the bridge Mike Jones had got caught in a whirlpool and it had taken him several minutes to get out.

The team met at the bridge. The canoeing was easier now, but there were other problems. Bandits shot at them once, but they were moving too fast. Crocodiles were a real danger, and one day Dave had to abandon his canoe to escape. Fortunately Steve had his gun ready, so he shot the crocodile and got Dave's canoe back.

They finally arrived at the Shafartak Bridge, tired and very tense, on 12th September.

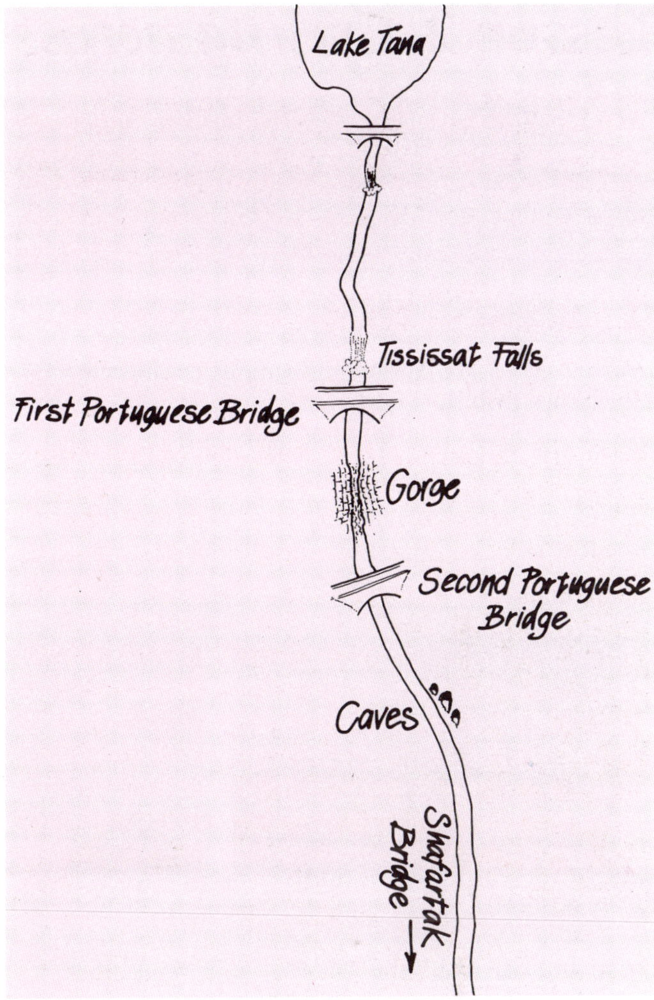

5

Read your story again and complete the table.

Expedition year	
Expedition leader	
Number of people	
Starting date	
Finishing date	
Number of deaths	

Homework

You were on the expedition you read about. Write a page from your expedition diary.

6

Work in pairs and discuss these questions.

Which expedition took place first?
Which expedition had more people?
Which expedition took longer?
Which expedition was more dangerous? Why?
Which expedition was more successful? Why?
Which expedition would you prefer to have been on? Why?

Language Summary

too and *enough*

The water was **too** fast and dangerous for the dinghies.
Dave and Steve didn't think it was safe **enough** to continue.

Past perfect

Once the team **had passed** the falls, they put the dinghies back on the river.

see practice page 93

Lesson 2 *Cycling across the Andes*

Language focus: *have to* and *must* for obligation

Skills focus: Listening and reading for main ideas and detail
Speaking: planning an adventure trip

a

b

1

Work in pairs. Match the photographs of different landscapes with the vocabulary.

1 beaches ___*c*___
2 glaciers ________
3 industrial ________
4 mountains ________
5 salt flats ________
6 vineyards ________
7 volcanoes ________

c

d

e

f

g

2

What and where are the Andes? Which landscapes would you expect to see when crossing the Andes? Compare your answers with another pair.

3

In 1991 Eric and Lina completed the first off-road crossing of the Andes by bicycle. Listen to the interview with Eric and tick the landscapes he mentions. Did any surprise you?

4

Listen to Eric again and complete the table.

Starting date: *August 1990*	Finishing date:
Highest altitude:	Lowest altitude:
Length of time in Bolivia: Chile: Argentina:	
Total distance travelled:	

5

Work in groups. Make a list of the problems you think Eric and Lina had.

Think about the weather, the different landscapes, other people, food and water, clothes, the cycling, camping.

6

Read part of an interview with Lina and Eric from a magazine article. Were any of your predictions correct?

'... well obviously there were the physical problems – we got very physically and mentally tired. The weather varied too – it was very hot in the desert during the day and freezing cold in the mountains at night. On the positive side, we didn't have to worry about wild animals. There were also the psychological difficulties of being with the same person 24 hours a day for seven months. But most of the problems were technical – punctures, for example, because we discovered that bicycle pumps don't work at high altitude. Then there's the problem of water. You have to calculate exactly how much water you need in the desert because it is very heavy to carry. We needed twelve litres each per day. But we didn't have to worry so much about food. Up in the mountains you mustn't get up too late because you have to cross rivers before 8am while they are still frozen. If we arrived late at a river, we had to carry the bikes through icy water ...'

7

Look at the article again. Which of the statements below are true, and which are false?

1 There were extreme temperatures. *T*
2 Lina and Eric's main problems were psychological. ___
3 They did the whole journey together. ___
4 Bicycle pumps work well at high altitude. ___
5 They didn't have enough food in the desert. ___
6 They needed twenty-four litres of water each day between them. ___
7 In the mountains the rivers froze at night. ___

8

Read the notes made from an interview with Lina and match the notes with the headings.

1 seeing the view at the end of the journey
2 running out of water in the desert
3 to cycle from Mongolia to Afghanistan
4 when we heard gun shots one night near the tent

Best moment ___ Biggest fear ___
Worst moment ___ Future plans ___

Now listen to Eric and make notes using the same headings.

9

Work in groups. Plan an adventure trip. Where would you go? What would you see and do? Name six essential pieces of equipment you would take with you.

Now tell your plans to another group.

Homework

Write a short summary of Lina and Eric's journey for the first part of the magazine article in Activity 6.
Begin:

Lina and Eric's epic journey started in ... . First they cycled through ...

Language Summary

have to and *must* for obligation
You **have to** calculate exactly how much water you need in the desert.
You **must** write a book about your trip.

Revision of the *-ing* form
We cycled past glaciers and saw them **crashing** into lakes.

see practice page 94

Lesson 3 *Organizing an expedition*

Language focus: Revision of future forms
Skills focus: Speaking: discussing and organizing an expedition
Writing a formal letter

1

Read this newspaper advertisement. Who put the advertisement in the paper? What is it for? Who do the advertisers want to hear from?

- *Going on an expedition?*
- *Need sponsorship?*
- *Then send details to Adventure Foundation.*

We'll give your expedition serious consideration.

The Adventure Foundation Trust
12 Enfield Street,
London W3

The Adventure Foundation Trust

2

Read the four letters asking for sponsorship for an expedition. Match the letters with the expeditions listed below.

1 A historical expedition. __________

2 Finding a cure for a disease. __________

3 A study of a rare animal. __________

4 A study of ice movements. __________

Which expedition sounds most interesting. Why?

A

16 Darwin Street
Brisbane
Australia

Dear Sir or Madam,

We should like to apply to your foundation for sponsorship for our expedition. We are planning a three-month trip to Vietnam to study the Snow Leopard. At the same time we are going to do some plant studies for the local university. There will be eight of us and we all have expedition experience. The cost of the expedition will be £15,000-£20,000, including air fares, transport etc.

Please help us.

Yours faithfully,

Alick Patterson

Alick Patterson

B

ALDBURY SCIENTIFIC UNIT
121 New Road LONDON SW2

The Adventure Foundation Trust
12 Enfield Street
LONDON W3

To the Adventure Foundation Trust,

Our unit is sending a four-month expedition to Antarctica next Spring. A team of 12 scientists is travelling to measure movements in the ice. This research is very important because it will help us to see how the earth's climate is changing.

Unfortunately the expedition will be expensive – about £35,000, including transport, scientific equipment and food. However we hope you will be able to support us.

Thanks

Dr Marcia Vitteri

Dr Marcia Vitteri

C

The Greco-Roman Institute

The Adventure Foundation Trust
12 Enfield Street
LONDON W3

July 1995

Dear Adventure Foundation Trust,

We would like to tell you about our expedition. We are a team of six archaeologists who are going to fly to Libya some time next year. We hope to help local archaeologists who have recently discovered the remains of an ancient Greek city, which may give us very valuable information about what life was like in ancient times. If the expedition is approved we will need between £20,000 – £25,000. The expedition will probably last approximately two months. The BBC are going to come out to make a documentary film about the excavation.

We hope you will give our expedition serious consideration.

Yours hopefully,

Lucia di Vicenza

Signora Lucia di Vicenza, Expedition Secretary

The Greco-Roman Institute,
Via Roma 102,
Rome, Italy.

D

Geneva Science Institute

1103 Geneva

18 June 1995

Can you help us with our expedition? We hope to go to India next year. We have been invited by the Indian government to help in research to find a cure for leprosy. The Indian Government have provided the cost of the air fares but we will need approximately £20,000 to cover all our other expenses. We are meeting officials from the Indian Government next Thursday so we will be able to give you more information then. At the moment we think we are going to send a team of about ten scientists and ten medical doctors.

Yours,

P Lesage

Pierre Lesage

3

Work in groups. You work for The Adventure Foundation Trust. Which expedition would you sponsor? Think about the following questions:

- Where is the expedition going?
- How long for?
- How many people are going to go?
- How practical is the expedition?
- What is the purpose of the expedition?
- How much will it cost?
- How well organized is it?

4

Now plan your group expedition. Make notes about it using the questions in Activity 3 to help you.

Example

Destination: Iceland
Purpose: to study volcanic activity
Duration of expedition: 2 months

Homework

Write the Adventure Foundation Trust's letter of reply to the expedition you decided to sponsor in Activity 3.

5

Look at the letters again. Which letter has the most appropriate ...

- address layout?
- date?
- greeting?
- first sentence?
- last sentence?
- ending?

6

In your group write a letter to The Adventure Foundation Trust asking for sponsorship.

Language Summary

Revision of future forms

Present continuous
Our unit **is sending** a four-month expedition to Antarctica next spring.

going to:
We are a team of six scientists who **are going** to visit Libya some time next year.

will
Unfortunately the expedition **will** be expensive

hope to and *hope (that)*
We **hope to** go to India next year.
We **hope** (**that**) you will be able to support us.

see practice page 95

Unit 1 Lesson 1

Language Summary 1

Prepositions of time

on *the wedding day*
at *lunch time*
in *the afternoon.*

We use ***at*** with times – eg ***two o'clock, lunch-time***; holidays – eg ***Christmas***; and ***night, midday*** and ***midnight***.

We use ***on*** with days and day + part of a day – eg ***Tuesday morning*** and dates – eg ***4th July***.

We use ***in*** with parts of the day – eg ***the afternoon***; years – eg ***2000***; months – eg ***January***; seasons – eg ***summer***, and to say when something will happen in the future – eg ***I'm going on holiday in two weeks***.

There is no preposition before ***this, next*** and ***last*** – eg ***this week, next year, last month***.

1

Complete the time expressions using *in, on* or *at*.

1 ____ spring
2 ____ Christmas
3 ____ 5 pm
4 ____ Tuesday
5 ____ Monday morning
6 ____ 1994
7 ____ March
8 ____ the New Year
9 ____ Easter
10 ____ midnight
11 ____ the weekend
12 ____ 18th June
13 ____ the 1970s
14 ____ the evening
15 ____ winter

Language Summary 2

Present simple

The bride ***dresses*** in traditional Thai costume.
The bridegroom usually ***wears*** a western-style suit.

The present simple is the infinitive of a verb without *to*. After the third person singular (*he, she* and *it*) we add **-s** – eg *wear* → *wears* or **-es** if the verb already ends in ***s*** – eg *dress* → *dresses*.

We usually make negative sentences with ***do/does*** + ***not*** before the main verb in the sentence – eg *The bridegroom* ***doesn't wear*** *a ring*.

We can make present simple questions with ***do/does*** before the subject – eg ***Does the bridegroom wear*** *a ring?* Or we can use a question word – eg ***What*** *do the bride and bridegroom wear?*

We use the present simple to talk about facts and things that are generally true or usually happen. We can also use it to talk about routines – things that we do every day.

2

Complete the text about this American festival using a preposition or the present simple of the verbs in brackets.

Thanksgiving

Thanksgiving ___*is*___ a festival which (2) ________ (take place) in the United States and Canada. The festival (3) ________ (give) thanks for the harvest and (4) ________ (celebrate) the first harvest of the Pilgrim Fathers (5) ________ 1621. In the United States, Thanksgiving (6) ________ (be) (7) ________ the autumn (8) ________ the last Thursday (9) ________ November, but in Canada it (10) ________ (be) (11) ________ October.

Thanksgiving (12) ________ (be) a big family holiday, when families (13) ________ (come) together and (14) ________ (have) a special meal. Some people (15) ________ (travel) hundreds of miles to be with their families. (16) ________ Thanksgiving, people (17) ________ (not have) lunch; they (18) ________ (have) a big dinner (19) ________ the evening or (20) ________ night. They (21) ________ (eat) very traditional food. Everyone (22) ________ (eat) turkey and there (23) ________ (be) vegetables like potatoes and sweet potatoes. The traditional dessert (24) ________ (be) pumpkin pie.

Some families (25) ________ (play) games together, like football or baseball, but others just (26) ________ (talk). (27) ________ the weekend a lot of people (28) ________ (go) to football matches or (29) ________ (watch) football on TV. They (30) ________ (not have) another dinner – they (31) ________ (eat) popcorn and (32) ________ (drink) beer!

Vocabulary

3

Anagrams are puzzles where the letters of a word are mixed up – eg ECKA is an anagram of CAKE.

These words are all in the lesson. What are they?

1 NIRG
2 LOEWSFR
3 DREIB
4 GDIDWNE
5 ESPTNESR
6 YEMCRENO

Language Summary

Present simple passive

When the eggs break, they ***are eaten****.*
Money ***is collected*** *and children* ***are chased*** *by the horse.*

Compare these two sentences:
The horse ***chases*** *children.* (active)
Children ***are chased*** *by the horse.* (passive)

There is no difference in meaning between the passive and active sentence. We use the passive when we want to focus on the object in the active sentence – eg *the eggs, money, children*. It is often not necessary to say who or what did the activity, but we can say who or what by using ***by*** **+ the agent** (*by the horse*).

We make the passive with ***is/are*** **+ the past participle of the verb**. For regular verbs, we make the past participle by adding **-ed** – eg *collect* → *collect****ed***.
Many verbs are irregular – eg *eat* → ***eaten***.

1

Read this text about making wine.

Do you like drinking wine? I do. It's my favourite drink, red or white!

Wine growers all over the world produce wine but I prefer Chilean wine. The wine making process can take years. Manufacturers grow their grapes in vineyards. When they are ripe, workers pick the grapes and take them to the winery. Machines press the grapes and pour the grape juice into barrels. The wine experts add sugar to help the fermentation, and then leave the wine, sometimes for several years. When it is ready, machines bottle the wine and the company sells it to wine dealers. The dealers distribute the cases of wine to shops and businesses, and wine lovers all over the world drink the final product. The year in which the wine was made is called the vintage. Some years produce excellent wines – they say it all depends on the weather! Cheers!

Complete the sentences below using the underlined verbs from the text. Use the present simple passive. The past participles you need are in the box.

added	bottled	distributed	drunk	grown	left
picked	poured	pressed	~~produced~~	sold	taken

1 Wine *is produced* all over the world.
2 The grapes ________ in vineyards.
3 The grapes ________ when they are ripe.
4 They ________ to the winery.
5 Then the grapes ________
6 The grape juice ________ into barrels.
7 Sugar ________ to help fermentation.
8 The wine ________ for several years.
9 When ready, the wine ________.
10 The bottles ________ to the wine dealers.
11 The cases of wine ________ to shops and businesses.
12 The final product ________ all over the world.

2

Now write questions for the statements in exercise 1.

1 *Where is wine produced* ?
2 *Where are the grapes* ?
3 *When* ?
4 ________ ?
5 ________ ?
6 ________ ?
7 ________ ?
8 ________ ?
9 ________ ?
10 ________ ?
11 ________ ?
12 ________ ?

Vocabulary

3

Fill in the two missing letters which complete the two words.

1 P A G *A* *N* O T H E R
2 F E S T I V ___ ___ W A Y S
3 L I ___ ___ M A L E
4 C A S T ___ ___ T T E R
5 C O S T U ___ ___ N
6 T O R ___ ___ U R C H

Language Summary 1

Present continuous

She**'s holding** something in her hand.

Is she **laughing**?

We make the present continuous with *is*/*are* + **verb** + ***-ing***.

We can use the present continuous to talk about something that is happening at or around the same time that we are speaking.

1

Look at the picture of this family. Write sentences about what is happening using the prompts.

1 father/pour/wine/glass *The father is pouring some wine into a glass.*

2 girl/drink/wine

3 grandmother/pass/bread/mother

4 mother/take/bread/

5 young man/feed/baby

6 dog/take/chicken/plate

2

Now anwer these questions about the picture.

1 What is the girl drinking? *She is drinking some wine.*

2 Are they eating fish?

3 What are the parents drinking?

4 Is the grandmother sitting down?

5 What's the baby doing?

6 Is the young man eating?

Language Summary 2

Present continuous for future social arrangements

*I'm so pleased that you**'re visiting** us next month.*

We can use the present continuous to talk about definite future social arrangements, such as the arrangements you write in your diary.

We often use a time clause with the present continuous – eg ***next month***.

3

Look at Kate's diary and write her arrangements for next week. Use the present continuous of the verbs in brackets.

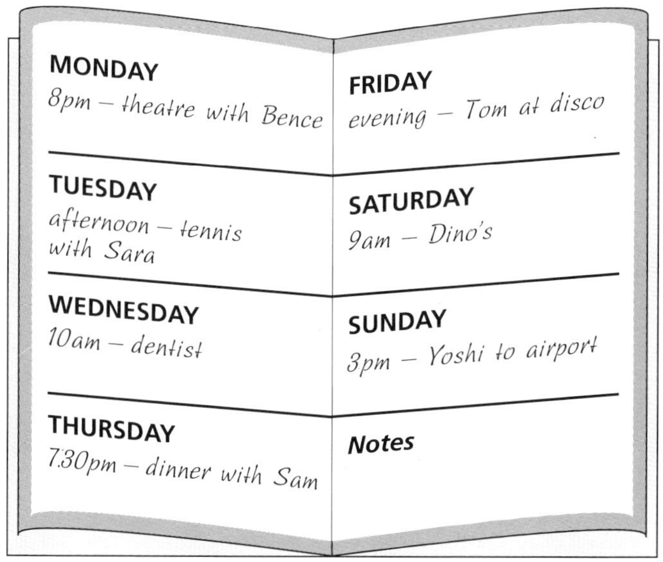

1 (go) *On Monday at 8pm she's going to the theatre with Bence.*

2 (play)

3 (go)

4 (have)

5 (meet)

6 (work)

7 (take)

4

What are you doing next week? Look at your diary and write five sentences using the present continuous. Use a different verb for each sentence.

eg *On Monday evening I'm having dinner with Vicky.*

1

2

3

4

5

Unit 2 Lesson 1

Language Summary 1

Wh- questions

***Where** can you buy the best travel books?*

Wh- questions start with ***What ...?, When ...?, Where ...?, Which ...?, Who ...?, Whose ...?, Why ...? How ...?***

We make **Wh- questions** like this:

Where	***can***	***you***	***buy***	*the best travel books?*
Wh- word +	auxiliary +	subject +	infinitive	(+ direct object)

***Who serves real Italian ice cream** in Covent Garden?*

If the ***Wh-*** word is the subject of the question we do not use an auxiliary verb and the word order is different: ***Wh-*** word + verb + object.

1

Make questions from these words.

1 What/time/does/close/Theatre Museum/the? *What time does the Theatre Museum close?*
2 What/this/size/is/T-shirt? ______
3 Where/bookshop/find/can/the/I/nearest? ______
4 Who/is/the/museum/to/going? ______
5 Why/want/of/map/Africa/you/a/do? ______
6 Whose/this/poster/is? ______
7 Which/you/pizza/like/would? ______
8 Who/an/ice/wants/cream? ______

2

Ask questions about the statements using Who or What.

1 Someone telephoned me yesterday. *Who telephoned you yesterday?*
2 I met someone at the theatre. *Who did you meet at the theatre?*
3 Someone gave me a free ticket. *Who* ______
4 We saw a ballet at Covent Garden. *What ballet* ______
5 Something happened during the performance. *What* ______
6 They found something. ______

Language Summary 2

Countable and uncountable nouns

***How many shops** are open on Sundays?*
***How much money** can you save at The Italian Connection?*

We use ***How many*** before countable nouns – eg *shops.*
We use ***How much*** before uncountable nouns – eg *money.*

3

Put the nouns in the box into the correct column in the table. Add some more words you know.

~~beer~~ ~~books~~ food hours information maps museums pasta theatres videos wine

countable	uncountable
books	beer

4

Dieter is shopping in Covent Garden.

Write the shop assistant's questions about the things he wants to buy using *How much* or *How many*. Then choose the correct answer from the phrases in the box.

one blue one ~~one bottle~~ one can one packet two ~~24 exposures~~ two bars two slices six

1 *How much mineral water would you like? One bottle please.*
2 *How many films would you like? 24 exposures please.*
3 ______
4 ______
5 ______
6 ______
7 ______
8 ______

Vocabulary

1

Find nine materials in the word square. All the words are in the lesson.

X	Z	S	I	L	K	O	P
P	O	T	T	E	R	Y	L
C	C	G	L	A	S	S	A
O	A	M	E	T	A	L	S
T	N	J	O	H	L	P	T
T	V	X	F	E	Y	Q	I
O	A	C	V	R	B	N	C
N	S	I	L	V	E	R	X

Language Summary 1

Order of adjectives

Indian silk and cotton *waistcoat.*

In descriptions, adjectives usually follow this order:

size colour origin material noun

Multicoloured African glass *necklace*

Any additional information goes at the end of the sentence.

2

Make sentences from these words.

1 suitcase/English/large/brown/leather/A

A large, brown English leather suitcase

2 Indian/A/blue/shirt/long

____

3 green/small/A/car/with a sun roof/Italian

____

4 large/Chinese/A/calendar/red and gold

____

5 American/A/steel/tennis racquet/black

____

6 with a shoulder strap/leather/An/Italian/handbag

____

7 computer/A/with a laser printer/small/Japanese/

____

8 pair of/Swiss/A/sunglasses/small

____

3

Write the descriptions for five things you have at home.

eg *A large, white, woollen rug from Greece.*

1 ____________________________

2 ____________________________

3 ____________________________

4 ____________________________

5 ____________________________

Language Summary 2

Yes/No **questions**

Is *it made of plastic?*

Statement	Question	Answer
It's made of plastic.	***Is it made of plastic?***	***Yes, it is./ No, it isn't.***

We make ***Yes/No*** **questions** with *be, have got* and auxiliary verbs (eg *can*) by changing the order of the subject and verb.

Do you use it in the bathroom?

Statement	Question	Answer
You use it in the bathroom.	***Do you use it in the bathroom?***	***Yes, you do./ No, you don't.***

We make ***Yes/No*** **questions** with other verbs by adding **Do** or **Does** at the beginning.

4

Can you guess what this household object is? Write the questions using the prompts. The answers will help you.

1 made/plastic? *Is it made of plastic?* No, it isn't.

2 made/glass? ____________ Yes, most of it.

3 anyone/use/it? ____________ Yes, they can.

4 round? ____________ Yes, sometimes.

5 square? ____________ Yes, sometimes.

6 mechanical? ____________ No, it isn't.

7 make/noise? ____________ No, it doesn't.

8 use/outside? ____________ Yes, you can, but not usually.

9 use/anytime? ____________ Yes, you can, but especially in the morning.

10 usually/bathroom? ____________ Yes, it is.

What is it? ____________

Unit 2 Lesson 3

Language Summary 1

First conditional

***If** you eat Garden Farm low fat margarine, you **will be** healthier.*
or
*You **will be** healthier **if** you **eat** Garden Farm low fat margarine.*

We make the first conditional with:

If + present simple + *will* + infinitive without *to*
if clause + main clause

or *Will* + infinitive without to + *if* + present simple
main clause + *if* clause

The *if* clause can come before or after the main clause, but when the *if* clause is first we write a comma (,) before the main clause.

We use the first conditional to talk about something that is possible in the future.

1

Complete the sentences using the correct form of the verb in brackets.

1 If you *use* (use) 'Gleam' shampoo, your hair *will be* (be) softer.
2 Your car __________ (go) faster if you __________ (use) 'Panther Oil'.
3 You __________ (have) healthier teeth if you __________ (brush) your teeth with 'All-White' toothpaste.
4 If you __________ (look) carefully, you __________ (see) all the animals in the Wildlife Park.
5 We __________ (give) you 10% off the price of your holiday if you __________ (book) it this month.
6 If you __________ (buy) three books, we __________ (give) you one free.

2

Complete these sentences.

eg 1 If I don't do my homework *my teacher won't be pleased.*
2 I will miss the beginning of my class __________________________
3 If I finish the book I am reading __________________________
4 If I can't sleep tonight __________________________
5 I will phone you __________________________
6 If I don't learn English __________________________

Language Summary 2

Comparative adjectives

*Now that summer is here and the weather is **sunnier**.*
*Always wanted to go somewhere **more exciting** than Europe?*

We add **-er** to one-syllable adjectives to make the comparative form – eg *fast* → *faster*.

If a one- or two-syllable adjective ends in **-y**, we change the **y** to an **i** before adding **-er** – eg *healthy* → *health**ier***.

If an adjective ends in **-e**, we just add **-r** – eg *wide* → *wider*.

If a one-syllable adjective ends in a vowel + one consonant, we double the final consonant before adding **-er** – eg *big* → *bigger*.

For most adjectives that are two syllables or more, we add **more** before the adjective – eg *interesting* → *more interesting*.

Some adjectives are irregular – eg *bad* → ***worse***, *good* → ***better***.

3

Complete the sentences using the comparative form of the words in brackets.

1 Wool is *warmer* (warm) than cotton.
2 Melons are __________ (expensive) than pears.
3 A holiday in Greece is __________ (cheap) than a holiday in Switzerland.
4 Glass is __________ (heavy) than plastic.
5 Planes are __________ (quick) than trains.
6 You can buy __________ (unusual) things in a market than in a shopping centre.
7 Supermarkets are __________ (convenient) than small shops.
8 Fruit is __________ (good) for you than chocolate.

Vocabulary

4

Compound nouns

Compound nouns are when two words are used together to make one noun. Some compound nouns are one word and some are two words.

Join one word from each column below to make six compound nouns from the lesson.

dish	dresser	__________
alarm	centre	__________
leisure	washer	*dishwasher*
travel	park	__________
hair	clock	__________
wildlife	agents	__________

Unit 3 Lesson 1

Language Summary 1

Superlative adjectives

*Santa Cruz is **the** second **largest** island in the Galapagos.*
*The Galapagos are one of **the most expensive** places in the world to visit.*

We add ***-est*** to one-syllable adjectives to make the superlative form – eg *cold* → *colder* → *cold**est**.*
If a one- or two-syllable adjective ends in ***-y***, we change the ***y*** to an ***i*** before adding ***-est*** –
eg *sunny* → *sunnier* → *sunn**iest**.*
If an adjective ends in ***-e***, we just add ***-st*** –
eg *large* → *larger* → *larg**est**.*
If a one-syllable adjective ends in a vowel + one consonant, we double the final consonant before adding ***-est*** –
eg *wet* → *wetter* → *wet**test**.*
For most adjectives that are two syllables or more, we add ***most*** before the adjective –
eg *expensive* → *more expensive* → ***most*** *expensive.*
Some adjectives are irregular –
eg *bad* → *worse* → ***worst***, *good* → *better* → ***best***.

1

Comparative or superlative?

Complete the sentences using the correct form of the words in brackets.

1 Greenland is the *largest* (large) island in the world.
2 Travelling by plane is *faster* (fast) than travelling by train.
3 Boracay Island in the Philippines has ______ (good) beaches I have ever seen.
4 Jamaica is ______ (sunny) than Norway.
5 Fjordland in New Zealand is ______ (wet) place in the world
6 Rain in the wet season is ______ (heavy) than during the rest of the year.
7 Easter Island is ______ (interesting) island I have ever visited.
8 A holiday in Thailand is ______ (exciting) than a holiday in Spain.

Language Summary 2

Definite and indefinite articles

The *Galapagos are* ***an*** *isolated group of volcanic islands on* ***the*** *Equator.*
A *Bishop from Panama discovered* ***the*** *Galapagos islands in 1535.*

The is the definite article. We use ***the*** when we are talking about a particular person or thing.

A and ***an*** are indefinite articles. We use them when it is not important to say which person or thing we are talking about. We use ***a*** before a consonant sound – eg ***a*** *tortoise* – and ***an*** before a vowel sound – eg ***an*** *island.*

2

Complete the gaps in the text with *a* or *the*.

This winter I had (1) *a* wonderful holiday on (2) ______ beach in the Galapagos. (3) ______ holiday was for three weeks. (4) ______ best beach was on Santa Cruz island, and I stayed at (5) ______ small hotel opposite (6) ______ church. (7) ______ hotel was run by (8) ______ family with four children, so it was quite noisy sometimes! Everyone went to church on Sundays. (9) ______ island was very beautiful and I swam and went for long walks on (10) ______ beach.

3

Complete the gaps in the text with *a*, *an* or *the*. Write – where no article is necessary.

1 Ecuador is near ______ Peru.
2 'Which postcard do you like?' '______ one of the giant tortoise.'
3 I think there's ______ post-office in Puerto Ayura.
4 ______ post office is next to ______ cinema.
5 Have you ever been to ______ South America?
6 Santa Cruz is ______ interesting island to visit.
7 Sheika Gonzalez is ______ naturalist guide.
8 ______ Lake Darwin is on Santa Cruz island.
9 I went on ______ cruise to ______ Galapagos ______ last year.
10 I like ______ nature.

4

Rewrite the following text with the correct punctuation and capital letters where necessary.

we went to australia last year to visit sharons family it was lovely especially the beaches near the capital city sydney after a few days in the city we went to ayers rock in the centre of the country the rock is incredible its a holy place for the aborigines and it changes colour when the sun sets

Language Summary 1

Past simple

In 1971 the Robertsons ***decided*** *to sail around the world. They* ***sold*** *their farm and house and* ***bought*** *a yacht called 'The Lucette'.*

We use the past simple to talk about completed actions which happened in the past.

To make the past simple of regular verbs we add ***-ed*** – eg *attack* → *attack**ed***. When the verb ends in ***-e***, we just add ***-d*** – eg *decide* → *decide**d*** . When the verb ends in ***-y*** we change the ***y*** to an ***i*** and add ***-ed*** – eg *dry* → *dr**ied***.

There are many irregular verbs in English – eg *buy* → ***bought***, *feel* → ***felt***.

1

Find the past tenses of these irregular verbs in the lesson and use them to complete the table.

present	past	present	past
be	was/were	know	
catch		light	lit
come		make	
cut		put	
eat		see	
feel		sell	
get		sink	
have		take	

2

Complete the sentences using the simple past of the verbs in brackets. Use the story in the lesson to help you.

1 In 1971 the Robinson family *sold their house and farm* . (sell)

2 They bought a yacht . (buy)

3 Whales made holes in the yacht . (make)

4 Water started to come in . (start)

5 Robin and Neil were seasick so Lyn gave them pills . (give)

6 Sandy caught their first fish . (catch)

7 They cut the fish up and cooked it in lemon juice . (cook)

8 The family ate raw fish when they had no more lemon . (eat)

9 The life raft was always wet so they so they moved into the rowing boat . (move)

10 Sharks followed them all the time . (follow)

11 The family felt . (feel)

12 Finally a Japanese fishing boat saw their flare . (see)

Language Summary 2

Pronunciation of regular verbs in the past simple

There are three different pronunciations of past simple endings for regular verbs.

We use \d\ when the verb ends with a voiced consonant – eg *follow* → *followed*.
We use \t\ when the verb ends with an unvoiced consonant – eg *attack* → *attacked*.
We use \Id\ when the verb ends with a d or a t – eg *start* → *started*.

3

Write the past simple of the regular verbs in the box and put them into the correct column according to their pronunciation.

Practise saying them aloud.

~~cook~~ correct decide dry happen invite kill like move pull survive talk watch

/d/	/t/	/Id/
dried	*cooked*	corrected
happened	liked	decided
killed	talked	invited
moved	watched	
pulled		
survived		

Vocabulary

4

Match the words from the lesson in A with their opposites in B.

A	B
after	go
buy	take
come	dry
give	cooked
happy	negative
positive	before
raw	sell
small	sad
wet	large

Language Summary 1

Prepositions of place

*The sharks are **at** South Point.*
*The volcano is **in the centre of** the island.*

We use prepositions of place to say WHERE things are.

1

Where's the cat? Write the prepositions of place under the correct diagrams.

above behind between in in the centre of in front of near next to on on the left of opposite ~~under~~

1 *under* 2 ______ 3 ______ 4 ______
5 ______ 6 ______ 7 ______ 8 ______
9 ______ 10 ______ 11 ______ 12 ______

2

Look at the picture below. Are the sentences true or false?

1 The fire is near the tree. *true*
2 The man is on the boat. ______
3 The dog is next to the man. ______
4 The snake is behind the tree. ______
5 The birds are in the hut. ______
6 The hut is in the centre of the island. ______

Language Summary 2

Future with *going to*

*We**'re going to live** in the north of the island.*
*We**'re going to catch** fish to eat.*

We use ***going to*** to talk about future intentions and plans, and to make predictions about future events from evidence we can see now –
eg *It's cloudy.* → *It's **going to** rain.*

We make the ***going to*** future with ***be*** + ***going to*** + **the infinitive of the verb**

3

What is Brett going to do next week? Write sentences.

1 get/haircut *He's going to get a haircut.*
2 buy/new clothes ______
3 have/job interview ______
4 visit/mother ______
5 write to/bank manager ______
6 go to/wedding ______
7 have dinner/some friends ______
8 play football/Saturday ______

What are you planning to do next week? Write five sentences.

eg *I'm going to play tennis on Sunday.*
1 ______
2 ______
3 ______
4 ______
5 ______

Pronunciation

4

Complete the list of nationalities. Then underline the stressed syllable. Use a dictionary to help you.

Country	Nationality
Jap<u>an</u>	Japan<u>ese</u>
Italy	
Germany	
Poland	
Scotland	
Norway	
Peru	
Australia	
Brazil	
America	

Language Summary 1

Present perfect simple

*We've **worked** together for five years now.*
*The band **has been** the most important thing in Cindy's life for a long time.*

We can use the present perfect simple to talk about something which began in the past and continues up to the present. We can also use it to talk about experiences – things we have done in our lives.

We make the present perfect simple with *have/has* + the past participle of the verb. For regular verbs, we make the past participle by adding ***-ed*** – eg *work* → *work**ed***. Many verbs are irregular – eg *be* → ***been***.

1

There are 15 verbs hidden in the word square. Find them and write them next to their past participles below. Some of the verbs are regular and some are irregular.

S	P	E	A	K	W	P
E	A	T	L	H	A	V
E	C	E	I	W	N	S
B	O	O	K	R	T	I
O	M	D	E	I	W	N
B	E	O	R	T	O	G
O	H	A	V	E	R	T
G	O	S	M	A	K	E

be	been		
______	booked	______	made
______	come	______	seen
______	done	______	sung
______	eaten	______	spoken
______	gone	______	wanted
______	had	______	worked
______	liked	______	written

2

Have you ever?

Write questions using *Have you ever* and the prompts. Then give true answers – *Yes, I have,* or *No, I haven't.*

eg **1** make/record *Have you ever made a record?*
No, I haven't.

2 write/song ______

3 eat/Chinese food ______

4 sing/group ______

5 be/on TV ______

6 speak to/pop star ______

7 play/guitar ______

8 see/pop concert ______

Language Summary 2

for* and *since

*We've only worked on my new song **for** two days.*
*We've wanted to make a record **since** we started the band.*

We can use ***for*** and ***since*** with the present perfect to say how long something has been happening.

We use ***for*** to talk about a period of time – eg *two days, five minutes, a long time.*
We use ***since*** to talk about a point in time – eg *we started the band, 6 o'clock, yesterday.*

3

Complete these sentences using for or since.

1. They have sung together *for* two years.
2. Lucy hasn't eaten Italian food *since* her holiday in Rome.
3. Lucy and Cindy have been friends ______ 1989.
4. Tony has liked Cindy ______ a long time.
5. Brock has been the band's agent ______ they started singing five years ago.
6. Cindy has enjoyed singing ______ she was a child.
7. I have been on holiday ______ two weeks.
8. Cindy hasn't seen Tony ______ last Friday.
9. Rob has been unhappy ______ weeks.
10. Tony hasn't spoken to Lucy ______ this morning.

Writing

4

Punctuate the conversation between Cindy and Tony.

Cindy: im so excited tony weve always wanted this chance is it really true or is it a dream

Tony: no cindy its not a dream weve always wanted to make a record and this time our dreams come true were going into the recording studio next week

Language Summary 1

should **for advice**

I think Cindy ***should*** *take a holiday.*
She ***shouldn't*** *stay at home all the time.*

We use ***should*** and ***shouldn't*** + **the infinitive without *to*** to say what we think is the right thing to do.

1

Read these three letters to the problem page of a magazine.
Match the letters with Auntie Pat's advice.

Dear Auntie Pat,
I've got a friend who is a singer but has not been successful. She wants to stop singing and get a job, but doesn't know what to do.

Dear Auntie Pat,
I don't know what to do. My friend sings in a band but one of the band members had a fatal accident and she blames herself for his death. What should I do?

Dear Auntie Pat,
My brother, Tony, wants my friend to sing in his band, but she doesn't want to. She wants to sing in another band. What should my brother do?

Auntie Pat's advice

A You should try to convince your friend that it's not her fault. ____

B Your brother should look for someone else to sing in his band. ____

C Your friend should get some professional careers advice. ____

Which letter did Lucy write?

2

Read about these people's problems. Write some advice for each problem using the pictures to help you.

1 *You should go to the cashpoint.*
2 *You shouldn't eat sweets.*
3 ______
4 ______
5 ______
6 ______

Language Summary 2

have got to **for obligation**

You'***ve got to*** start living again.
You'***ve got to*** help Tony.

We can use ***have to*** or ***have got to*** + a verb in the infinitive to express obligation or necessity. They both have the same meaning.

3

Make sentences with *have to* or *have got to* using the prompts below.

1 Tony/telephone Brock *Tony has got to telephone Brock.*
2 Brock/write/new contract ______
3 Tony and Cindy/go/recording studio ______
4 The police/interview Lucy ______
5 Cindy/meet Tony ______
6 Tony/find another person for the band ______

Now write three things you have got to do this weekend.

eg *I've got to cook dinner for my family on Saturday.*
1 ______
2 ______
3 ______

Language Summary 1

will for predictions

*He'**ll** be nervous on his own.*
*Cindy **won't** change her mind*

We use ***will/won't*** to make predictions about the future; to talk about things that will definitely happen or not happen or that we think will happen or not happen.

1

What do you think life will be like in the future?

Here is one person's opinion. Complete the paragraph using the correct form of the verbs in brackets.

In the future, we (1) *won't need* (need) newspapers because we (2) *will get* (get) all our news from the TV. Books (3) ________ (be) a thing of the past. Instead we (4) ________ (buy) cassettes of books to listen to. The weather (5) ________ (be) the same all year round because of the changes in climate, and people (6) ________ (lose) weight because there (7) ________ (be) as much food in the world. We (8) ________ (do) more sport because we (9) ________ (have) more free time. Everyone (10) ________ (feel) happier because we (11) ________ (have to) work as hard as we do now.

2

Do you agree with the opinion in exercise 1? Write a paragraph saying what YOU think life will be like in the future.

____
____
____
____

Pronunciation

3

Look at these pairs of words. If they have the same vowel sound write S; if they have a different vowel sound write D.

1 made grey *S*
2 house noise *D*
3 shop clock ________
4 talk bought ________
5 there hear ________
6 would wood ________
7 dark vase ________
8 glass black ________

Language Summary 2

Pronouns and possessive adjectives and pronouns

*I'm really pleased for **him**.* (= subject and object pronouns)

*I can't live without **your** love.* (= subject pronoun and possessive adjective)

4

Complete the table below.

subject pronouns	object pronouns	possessive adjectives	possessive pronouns
I		my	
	you		yours
he		his	
	her		hers
it		its	
	us		ours
they		their	

5

Choose the correct pronouns or possessive adjectives in these sentences.

1 'Is that your/yours guitar?' – 'No, this is my/mine. That one must be your/yours.'
2 'What's your/yours favourite pop group?' – 'Duo. Their/Theirs best song is *I can't live without your love*. Rob wrote it/its.'
3 'Is that Lucy's new car?' – 'No, that's not her/hers. Her/Hers car is black.'
4 'Have you seen Cindy and Tony?' – 'No, I haven't seen they/them for ages and I've lost their/theirs phone number. Have you got it/its?'
5 'Now that Cindy and Tony are famous, they/their are very rich.'

Vocabulary

6

Can you find the nine words in the puzzle?

They are all types of music or musical instruments.

S	D	C	Q	S	H	V
B	C	L	X	R	P	I
P	I	A	N	O	O	O
O	X	S	M	C	P	L
C	H	S	O	K	E	I
G	U	I	T	A	R	N
K	T	C	U	R	A	A
P	J	A	Z	Z	M	H
X	F	L	U	T	E	B

Language Summary 1

Zero conditional

***If** they **go** anywhere as a family, they **need** two cars.*
***If** I **bring** a friend home, I **get** five faces at the window.*

We make the zero conditional with:

If + present simple + present simple
if clause + main clause

The *if* clause can come before or after the main clause, but when the *if* clause is first we follow it with a comma (,).

We use this type of conditional to talk about habits or facts.

1

Read about the Astons' friend Alistair. Complete the text using the correct form of the phrases in the box.

be bad	be busy	be late	cycle to work
~~get up~~	go home	go to the park	have breakfast
have lunch	leave work	start work	

Alistair's day starts early. He (1) *gets up* at 6.30am, has a shower, and (2) ________ – usually bacon and eggs – before his two children get up. If he (3) ________, he just has coffee. After breakfast, he gets his bicycle out and (4) ________. It usually takes him half an hour. If the weather (5) ________, he takes the car. He (6) ________ at 8.00am. He sees clients in the morning, then (7) ________ at a Pizzeria at about one o'clock. If he (8) ________, he just has a sandwich in his office. The afternoon is usually full of meetings. He (9) ________ at about 4.00pm and meets the children at school. They often (10) ________ for an hour and play football if they are feeling energetic, but sometimes they just (11) ________.

2

Write sentences about Debra using the zero conditional.

1 sunny/I/take dogs/park *If it's sunny, I take the dogs to the park.*
2 weather/bad – I/stay/home ________
3 parents/go/holiday – I/look after/house ________
4 I/feel tired – I/not go/jogging ________
5 my friend Samina/stay – we/camping ________
6 weather/good – cycle/work ________

What do you do ... ?

eg 1 *If I am tired, I go to bed early.*
2 ... if you are tired? ________
3 ... if the weather's good? ________
4 ... if you feel angry? ________

Language Summary 2

Talking about advantages and disadvantages

***One disadvantage of being** an only child **is that** you can be lonely.*
***One advantage of being** an only child **is that** you get lots of presents.*

We can talk about advantages and disadvantages by saying ***One advantage/disadvantage of** + **-ing/noun** + **...** **is that ...***

3

Write one advantage and one disadvantage for the following

eg 1 eating out
One advantage of eating out is that there is no washing up.
One disadvantage of eating out is that it is expensive.

2 living in a city
____
____

3 working at night
____
____

4 travelling by bus
____
____

5 shopping at a market
____
____

Vocabulary

4

Rooms

Match the rooms of the house with the definitions.

bedroom	The smallest room in the house.
living room	The room where you sleep.
hall	The room where you eat your meals.
toilet	The TV is usually in this room.
dining room	You can have a shower here.
bathroom	The cooking is done here.
kitchen	The room near the front door.

Language Summary

be allowed and *could* for permission

*I **was allowed** to drink wine at dinner but I **wasn't allowed** to smoke.*
*I **could** eat sweets between meals.*

We can use **(*not*) *allowed* + infinitive with *to*** and ***could/couldn't* + infinitive without *to*** to talk about general permission in the past. We also use **(*not*) *allowed* + infinitive with *to*** to talk about permission for a particular occasion.

have to for obligation

I *didn't **have to** clean the house, but I **had to** clean my room.*

We use ***had to*** to talk about obligation in the past – to say when something was obligatory. We use ***didn't have to*** when something was NOT obligatory – it was optional.

1

Complete the conversation using the correct form of *could, allowed to* or *had to* and one of the verbs in the box.

be buy come do do ~~eat~~ go out go out help play visit watch

Brendan: My brother and I had quite a strict childhood. For example, we (1) *weren't allowed to eat* sweets between meals, but we didn't have any money to buy them anyway!

Jane: Well, we (2) ________ ________ sweets – we used our pocket money, but there were lots of things we (3) ________ ________: for example we (4) ________ ________ in the street or talk to people we didn't know.

Brendan: But were you (5) ________ ________ in the evenings?

Jane: Yes, but I (6) ________ ________ home by 10pm.

Brendan: That was no problem for me – I (7) ________ ________ in the evenings, and I (8) ________ ________ home at any particular time. But I (9) ________ ________ my homework first before I (10) ________ ________ my friends.

Jane: So did I. I hated doing my homework, but I always did it because then I (11) ________ ________ TV afterwards, or play football. Weekends were the best time because then we (12) ________ ________ with the housework – we could do what we liked.

2

Jane's cousins Sue and Dave had different rules when they were sixteen. What were they? Write sentences using *(not) be allowed/could/couldn't/had to/didn't have to.*

1 *Sue wasn't allowed to eat sweets.*
2 ________________________________
3 ________________________________
4 ________________________________
5 ________________________________
6 ________________________________

Vocabulary

3

***Make* or *do*?**
Put the phrases in the box in the correct column.

~~your bed~~ a cake the cooking your homework the ironing a mistake a noise the shopping a suggestion the washing the washing up

make	do
your bed	

4

Complete the conversation between Sue and Dave using the correct form of *make* or *do*.

Dave: It's your turn to (1) *do* the washing up.

Sue: But I did it this morning.

Dave: OK, I'll do it. But you'll have to (2) ________ the shopping.

Sue: That's fine. I quite like (3) ________ the shopping.

Dave: And when you come back we can (4) ________ the cooking together. Remember it's Salah's birthday and we promised to cook him dinner.

Sue: Are you going to (5) ________ a cake?

Dave: Well, I haven't really got time. I've got to (6) ________ the ironing as well.

Sue: OK, I was only (7) ________ a suggestion. Maybe I'll (8) ________ him one.

Unit 5 Lesson 3

Language Summary

Adverbs of frequency

The father ***usually*** *goes out to work.*
Marriage between people from different cultures is ***always*** *difficult.*

We usually put adverbs of frequency before the main verb, but after the verb *to be*.

Men ***don't usually*** *spend enough time with their children.*

When there are several parts to the verb we generally put the adverb after the first auxiliary verb.

1

Write the adverbs in the box on the scale in the correct order.

frequently occasionally often rarely sometimes usually

always | _ | _ | _ | _ | _ | _ | never

2

Rewrite the sentences below using the adverbs in brackets.

1 In Italy the woman does the housework. *In Italy the woman usually does the housework. (usually)*
2 In Italy a girl has to ask permission to go out. ________________ (often)
3 In Italy people get divorced. ________________ (rarely)
4 Parents in Norway are not strict. ________________ (usually)
5 Parents in Britain are strict ________________ (occasionally)
6 In Norway the father stays at home with the children. ________________ (sometimes)
7 In Britain couples do the shopping together. ________________ (frequently)
8 In Britain people don't get married in a church. ________________ (always)
9 People spend too much money on weddings. ________________ (frequently)
10 A second marriage lasts longer than a first marriage in Britain. ________________ (usually)

Now write three sentences about your own country.

1 ________________
2 ________________
3 ________________

3

Rewrite these sentences about Ida to make sentences with similar meanings.
Use adverbs of frequency.

1 When I get up late, I don't have breakfast.
When I get up late, I never have breakfast.
2 I visit my parents most Sundays.
____
3 I have been late for work a few times.
____
4 I have had to go to the doctor once or twice in my life.
____
5 My friend Mario is able to help me some of the time.
____
6 My sister can't afford to go on holiday most years.
____
7 When I was a child I was not allowed to play outside most of the time.
____
8 In my home town people went to Mass every Sunday.
____
9 I haven't tried to give up smoking more than once or twice.
____
10 I didn't make my bed when I was young.
____

Vocabulary

4

Complete the text using the words and phrases in the box. All the words and phrases are in the lesson.

breaks up children divorce family living together marriage married relatives

Although modern (1) __________ life in Britain is not as hard as it was, it can still be difficult. There are many decisions to make: whether or not to get (2) __________, for example. (3) __________ is still very popular, although people worry that the (4) __________ rate is very high. Couples who are not married but (5) __________ often have contracts in case the relationship (6) __________ later. Then there is also the decision of whether or not to have (7) __________. Another problem is that people are living longer and many families worry about how to care for elderly (8) __________.

Language Summary 1

Past continuous and past simple

*Sir Dennis **was** in the study. He **was lying** on the floor.*
*I **was reading** when I **heard** three shots.*

The past continuous describes an activity which was in progress at a specific time in the past.

We make the past continuous with the past tense of the verb to be **(*was/were*)** + **the *-ing*** form of the verb.

We use the past simple to talk about a completed action in the past (see Unit 3 Lesson 2).
We can use the past continuous and the past simple together to describe an activity or situation in the past which was interrupted by another action.

*I **was reading** when I **heard** three shots.*

1

Where were you? What were you doing? Write true sentences about yourself.

eg **1** At 10pm last night *I was in the living room. I was watching TV.*
2 At 1pm yesterday ________
3 At midnight last night I ________
4 Last Sunday evening I ________

Write three true sentences about somebody else.

eg *At 3pm yesterday my brother was at the airport. He was waiting for a flight to Madrid.*
1 ________
2 ________
3 ________

2

Past simple or past continuous?

Complete the conversation between Sherlock Holmes and Sir Dennis's gardener, Pierre, with the correct form of the verbs in brackets.

Holmes: What (1) *were you doing* (you/do) on the night of the murder?
Pierre: I (2) ________ (be) in the garden – I (3) ________ (work) near the lake until 9pm.
Holmes: (4) ________ (you/hear) anything strange?
Pierre: Well, I (5) ________ (hear) Lady Francesca and Sir Dennis. They (6) ________ (be) on the terrace and (7) ________ (argue) about something.
Holmes: Where (8) ________ (you/be) at 11.30pm?
Pierre: I (9) ________ (drink) beer in the kitchen when Lady Francesca (10) ________ (come/in). She (11) ________ (cry).

Language Summary 2

anybody, nobody, somebody, everybody

*There wasn't **anybody** else in the room.*
*I saw **somebody** in the summer-house.*

We usually use ***somebody*** in affirmative sentences and ***anybody*** in negative sentences and questions. We can say ***-body*** or ***-one*** – eg *every**one*** = ***everybody***.

3

This is a conversation between Sherlock Holmes and the local policeman about the murder of Sir Dennis. Complete the conversation with *anybody, nobody, somebody* or *everybody*.

Policeman: Who do you think murdered Sir Dennis?
Holmes: Well (1) *nobody* said very much but I'm sure (2) ________ is lying. Did (3) ________ look particularly nervous?
Policeman: No, (4) ________ looked calm.
Holmes: But you say (5) ________ had a reason to kill Sir Dennis.
Policeman: Yes, sir, that's right. (6) ________ liked him very much – he was very unpopular.
Holmes: Well, I suppose we'll have to interview (7) ________ again.

Vocabulary

4

Prepositions of direction
Match the prepositions in the box to the diagrams.

across	along	down	into	round	through	up

1 ________ 2 ________ 3 ________
4 ________ 5 ________ 6 ________ 7 ________

Complete the text with the correct prepositions.

The morning after the murder Sherlock Holmes started to look for the murder weapon. First he went (1) *into* the study and then (2) ________ the main stairs. He checked the bedrooms then went back (3) ________ the stairs and (4) ________ the dining room. Nothing. He went (5) ________ the lounge and out (6) ________ the garden. He walked (7) ________ the path to the summer-house, but it was locked. He walked (8) ________ the summer-house looking carefully in the grass. He went to the lake and walked (9) ________ it. Then he was sure; the murderer had thrown the gun (10) ________ the water!

Language Summary 1

Past simple passive

The Pyramids ***were built*** *thousands of years ago. Archaeologists are not totally sure how the Great Pyramid* ***was built****.*

The Egyptians ***built*** *the pyramids thousands of years ago. (active)*	*The Pyramids* ***were built*** *thousands of years ago by the Egyptians. (passive)*

There is no difference in meaning between the passive and the active, just a difference in focus. The object of the active sentence becomes the subject of the passive sentence – ie in the active sentence the focus is on *the Egyptians* and in the passive sentence the focus is on *the pyramids*.

We make the past simple passive with ***was/were*** + **the past participle of the verb**. (see Unit 1 Lesson 2).

1

Make sentences about how the pyramids were made. Use the prompts below.

1 site/pyramid/choose *The site for the pyramid was chosen*
2 site/make/flat ____________________
3 stone/cut/quarry ____________________
4 blocks/move/workers ____________________
5 stones/put/place ____________________

2

Now describe how the Statue of Liberty was made.

1 Statue of Liberty/suggest/Frenchman *The Statue of Liberty was suggested by a Frenchman*
2 Money/contribute/French ____________________
3 1885/stones/take apart ____________________
4 Stones/transport/New York ____________________
5 Stones/reassemble/New York ____________________
6 Base/make ____________________
7 Finally/statue/dedicate/President Cleveland/October 28th 1886 ____________________

Language Summary 2

Determiners: *some, a, an*

It contained ***a*** *broken wine bottle,* ***some*** *Victorian money and* ***a*** *newspaper.*

We use ***a*** and ***an*** before singular countable nouns – eg ***a wine bottle, an old time capsule***.

We use ***some*** before plural countable nouns – eg ***some wine bottles, some photographs*** and before uncountable nouns – eg ***some money, some information***.

3

Complete this conversation with *a, an* or *some*.

Joshua: What would you put in (1) *a* time-capsule?

Murat: Oh, I don't know ... How about (2) ____ TV?

Joshua: (3) ____ TV! That's (4) ____ silly suggestion – it's too big. (5) ____ calculator would be better, if you want (6) ____ example of modern technology.

Murat: Yes, but what about (7) ____ watch with a TV – you know the sort! That at least would be (8) ____ original idea.

Joshua: OK. I'd put in (9) ____ CDs of different types of music, and maybe (10) ____ magazine.

Murat: Yes, and how about (11) ____ toy cars, or even (12) ____ doll wearing the latest fashion!

Language Summary 1

Direct *Wh-* questions

What *does the word 'Olympiad' mean?*

Indirect *Wh-* questions

Do you know what *the word 'Olympiad' means?*

We make indirect questions with a phrase like ***Do you know*** or ***Can you tell me*** + ***Wh-* question word**. We do not use the auxiliary verb *do/does* and the word order is the same as it is in a statement.

eg ***Do you know what the word 'Olympiad' means?***
The word 'Olympiad' means ...

(See Unit 2 Lesson 1).

1

Write the direct and indirect questions for this interview with Carl Lewis using the prompts.

1 Where/born? *Where were you born?*
Can you tell me where you were born?

2 How many/brothers and sisters/have got? ______

3 When/start/running? ______

4 Why/become/athlete? ______

5 Who/hero? ______

6 When/win/four gold medals? ______

7 How often/train? ______

8 What/do/in/free time? ______

Think of two more questions you would like to ask Carl.

Write the direct and indirect forms for each question.

1 ______

2 ______

2

Now read the text about Carl Lewis and write his answers to questions 1 – 8.

Carl Lewis, one of the greatest athletes this century, was born in Alabama, USA, one of a family of four children. He started running at school. His parents and his athletics teacher knew that Carl had a special talent, and encouraged him to think seriously about becoming an athlete. His hero was Jesse Owens, the Olympic record holder. Carl equalled Owens' record by winning four gold medals at the 1984 Olympic Games. Carl trains for at least three hours a day, every day. His hobbies are basketball and pop music.

1 *I was born in Detroit, USA.*
2 ______
3 ______
4 ______
5 ______
6 ______
7 ______
8 ______

Vocabulary

3

Sport

Match the places and equipment with the sports to complete the table.

places

course court gym pitch pitch pool ring

equipment

club football gloves goggles racquet stick weights

sport	place	equipment
football	*pitch*	*football*
tennis		
golf		
weightlifting		
swimming		
hockey		
boxing		

Language Summary 1

Present perfect and past simple

*She's **collected** over 100 items.*
*She **started** her collection five years ago.*

We can use the **present perfect** to describe an activity or state which started in the past but continues in the present (see Unit 4, Lesson 1), or a completed state or activity which is important now.
We use the **past simple** to talk about a completed activity or state (see Unit 3, Lesson 2).
We use the **past simple + a time expression + *ago*** to count back in time from the present.

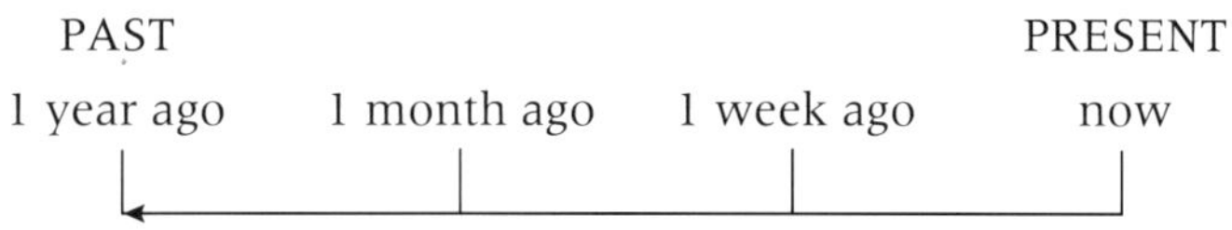

Language Summary 2

already, yet* and *just

*I've **already** collected over 100 things.*

We can use the present perfect with ***already*** to emphasize that something has happened before the time of speaking.

*We have not received permission to land **yet**.*

We usually use ***yet*** in negatives and questions to talk or ask about things we expect to happen.

*We have **just** landed at Loja airport.*

We can use the present perfect with ***just*** to say that something has happened very recently.

Already and ***just*** usually come before the main verb in the sentence. ***Yet*** usually comes at the end of the sentence.

1

Sandra's friend Denise is writing to her about Sandra's planned trip to Britain. Complete the letter using the present perfect or past simple of the verbs in brackets.

Dear Sandra,

I (1) *'ve just received* (just/receive) your letter. I'm so glad you're coming to visit us in Britain.

Rod and I (2) ________ (just/fly) back from a holiday in Malta. (3) ________ (you/collect) anything from Air Malta yet? If not, I've got a few things for you.
Anyway, what about your holiday? Is this the first time you (4) ________ (fly) Air France? We (5) ________ (go) on an Air France flight last year and I (6) ________ (think) they were really good. That's when I (7) ________ (get) you that spoon. You must have lots of spoons in your collection by now!
Anyway, I must stop writing now. I'll see you at the airport next week.

Love Denise.

2

Make sentences from these words using the present perfect. Put the words in brackets in the correct place in the sentence.

1 Sandra/collect/over 100 things/from aeroplanes. (already) *Sandra has already collected over 100 things from aeroplanes*
2 Sandra/write/Denise (just) ________
3 Sandra/not get/anything/Singapore Airlines. (yet) ________
4 Denise/give/Sandra/lots of things. (already) ________
5 Sandra/not collect/air ticket/ (yet) ________
6 Denise and Rod/be/holiday/Malta. (just) ________

Vocabulary

3

Travel

Complete the text with words from the box.

~~airport~~	check-in	departure lounge	duty free		
flight	luggage	passport	plane	ticket	took off

When I arrived at the (1) *airport* at 7 o'clock, there was a long queue at the (2) ________ desk. The attendant weighed my (3) ________ and looked at my (4) ________ to Miami. Then a customs official checked my (5) ________ before I went into the (6) ________. Next I bought some cheap whisky in the (7) ________ shop. Then they announced that my (8) ________ would be delayed. Two hours later we were called to Gate 2 and we got on the (9) ________. We finally (10) ________ at midnight!

Pronunciation

4

Each of the words in the first column contains a 'silent' letter or letters which are not pronounced. Circle the letter or letters. Then match the words in each column that rhyme (sound the same).

1 answer	die
2 wear	home
3 walk	where
4 know	dancer
5 why	white
6 comb	fork
7 brought	go
8 night	port

Unit 7 Lesson 2

Language Summary 1

Present perfect simple and present perfect continuous

How much TV ***have*** *you* ***watched*** *this week?*
I've ***been watching*** *more than usual this week*

We make the present perfect continuous with ***have/has*** + ***been*** + **the** ***-ing*** form of the verb. We use the present perfect continuous to talk about the duration of a state or activity when it is not important whether the state or activity has finished or not.

We use the present perfect simple when the state or activity is complete but the result is important now. (See Lesson 1 of this unit.)

1

Write sentences about Jacob and his brother Tim using the present perfect continuous.

1 Jacob/live/Liverpool/since/a child *Jacob has been living in Liverpool since he was a child.*
2 Jacob/collect bottles/ten years ________
3 Jacob and Tim/share/flat/two years ________
4 Jacob/study hard/this month ________
5 Jacob and Tim/argue a lot/recently ________
6 Jacob/go out with/Elena/two months ________
7 Tim feel ill/all weekend ________

2

Present perfect simple or present perfect continuous?

Complete the text about Janet using the most appropriate form of the verbs in brackets.

Janet (1) ________ (be) a market researcher for six years. During this time she (2) ________ (interview) over 60,000 people and (3) ________ (find out) a lot of interesting information. For the last eight months she (4) ________ (study) at night school. She (5) ________ (do) a management course there, which finishes in June.

'I feel I (6) ________ (have) enough of this job,' she says. 'It (7) ________ (be) good, but now it's time for a change. One reason is that for the last two years I (8) ________ (get up) at 6.30am every day to travel to work – it's very tiring. So I (9) ________ (apply for) jobs nearer home.'

Language Summary 2

Polite requests

Could *you spare a couple of minutes, please?*
May *I just ask a few questions?*
Would you mind *answering a few questions?*

We make polite requests with ***Could*** or ***May*** + **the infinitive** of the verb, or ***Would you mind*** + **the** ***-ing*** form of the verb.

3

Complete Janet's requests using ***May I ...?, Could I/you ...?*** **or** ***Would you mind ...?***

1 *Could you* tell me about your hobbies?
2 ________ borrow your pen?
3 ________ help me with this survey?
4 ________ filling in this questionnaire?
5 ________ helping us with our survey?
6 ________ ask you a few questions about your work?
7 ________ answer a few questions?
8 ________ giving us your opinion of this product?
9 ________ say which you prefer?
10 ________ spare a few minutes?

Vocabulary

4

Collocations

Match the nouns in the box with the verbs. There are two nouns for each verb.

a concert	dinner	for a drink	football
money	the news	the piano	a picnic
the radio	time	~~TV~~	for a walk

1 to watch *TV* ________
2 to listen to ________ ________
3 to have ________ ________
4 to go ________ ________
5 to play ________ ________
6 to spend ________ ________

Unit 7 Lesson 3

Language Summary

-ing form

Then she was right beside me, ***coming up*** *the pavement.*
They passed ***talking*** *nineteen to the dozen.*

We can use the ***-ing* form** when the subject of the main verb does or experiences two things at the same time – eg *He walked out of the house, singing to himself.* We can also use the ***-ing* form** to join two sentences together – eg *She saw the cat. It was playing in the garden. = She saw the cat playing in the garden.*

1

Match the two halves of the sentences.

1 Miranda came up the road, — b
2 The old women passed him,
3 Frederick couldn't concentrate,
4 A young boy passed,
5 Frederick could hear Miranda,
6 Frederick pushed Miranda in the van,
7 It was getting darker,

a talking to each other.
b singing to herself.
c thinking about Miranda.
d cycling fast.
e walking quickly.
f becoming difficult to see.
g closing the door behind her.

2

Complete the text using the *-ing* form of the verbs in the box.

bark	~~blow~~	feel	lie	put on
sing	talk	wear		

The wind grew stronger, (1) _blowing_ directly into Anna's face. She bent her head down and started to climb the hill, (2) __________ a song to herself. A dog ran across the road, (3) __________ loudly. She ignored it. Further up the hill two young girls cycled past, (4) __________ to each other. (5) __________ her hat, Anna turned into a side street; there was a strange dark object (6) __________ in the middle of the road and a man (7) __________ a blue coat, who was running towards the park. (8) __________ quite frightened, Anna ran over to see what the object was.

Vocabulary

3

Verbs of movement

Match the actions with the pictures.

bend down	climb up	jump	lie down
run	sit down	stand up	walk

1 __________

2 __________

3 __________

4 __________

5 __________
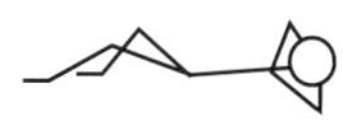
6 __________

7 __________

8 __________

4

Verbs of looking

Complete the sentences using the words in the box.

didn't see	look	looked	saw	saw
was staring	~~watch~~	watched		

1 _Watch_ out ! There's a car coming.
2 I __________ in the mirror and __________ that my hair was a mess.
3 I felt uncomfortable in the restaurant because the man opposite __________ at me.
4 I __________ a great film last week.
5 The police officer __________ the house all weekend, but __________ anything.
6 __________ what I've found!

Reading

5

Read the extract from 'The Collector'. Underline nine other differences between this extract and the original one on page 46.

Two old <u>men</u> with walking sticks (it began to snow again) appeared and came across the road towards me. It was just what I didn't want, I nearly gave up then and there, but I lay down, they passed laughing, I don't think they saw me or the bus. There were no cars parked anywhere in that district. Ten minutes passed. I got out and closed the back. It was all planned.

Language Summary

Making and replying to suggestions

Why don't we *watch the fireworks?*
Let's *go to a club.*
Shall *we go to the cinema?*

We can make suggestions using ***Why don't you/we, Let's*** or ***Shall we*** + **the infinitive without *to*.**

How about *some spaghetti?*
What about going *Scottish dancing?*

We can also make suggestions using ***How/What* about** + **noun** or + **the *-ing*** form of the verb.

There are lots of phrases we can use to accept or reject suggestions. Eg – to accept – ***That's a good idea.*** or ***OK, fine***. or to reject – eg ***Sorry/I'm afraid I can't. (I'm busy.)*** or ***Well, I'd prefer to do something different***.

1

Complete the conversation by making suggestions using the correct form of the verbs in brackets.

Jo: What *about playing* (play) tennis tomorrow night?

Sam: Sorry, I can't. I'm going Scottish dancing at the festival. Why (1) ____________ (come) too? And how (2) ____________ (go) to see a film on Wednesday as well?

Jo: OK, but the origami class is on Wednesday too. Shall (3) ____________ (try) that first?

Sam: That's a good idea. Oh, look. Here's Fabio.

Fabio: Hi! Listen, I've got an idea. Why (4) ____________ (go) Scottish dancing tomorrow night?

Sam: We're already going. Let (5) ____________ (meet) for a drink first.

Fabio: I'm afraid I can't. I work late on Mondays. Shall (6) ____________ (meet) at the hall?

Sam: Well, I'd still like to go for a drink, Jo, so what (7) ____________ (go) to the Blue Flamingo? Say, seven o'clock?

Jo: Great! And why (8) ____________ (go) back to my house after the dancing and watch a video?

2

Write suggestions using the prompts. Then write replies to the suggestions.

1 tonight **2** weekend **3** this afternoon **4** now

5 tomorrow **6** Thursday **7** Friday **8** next summer

1 *Why don't we go running tonight?* ____ *OK*
2 ____________________ ____________
3 ____________________ ____________
4 ____________________ ____________
5 ____________________ ____________
6 ____________________ ____________
7 ____________________ ____________
8 ____________________ ____________

Write two more suggestions and replies to them.

____

____

Vocabulary

3

Entertainment

Put the words in the box in the table. Some words can go in more than one column.

actor audience band box office
concert marathon play player referee
singer spectator ticket

Theatre	Music	Sport
actor		

Now complete the text using words from the table.

Yesterday I went to a (1) *concert* . A local (2) ____________ were playing and they weren't very good. The (3) ____________ was too loud and the guitarist was not very experienced. Anyway, the rest of the (4) ____________ seemed to enjoy it, so perhaps it was just me.

Tomorrow I'm going to the theatre to see a (5) ____________ . My favourite (6) ____________ is in it. I'm just going to phone the (7) ____________ to see if they've got any (8) ____________ left.

Unit 8 Lesson 2

Language Summary 1

Non-defining relative clauses

This is me on the top of Mount Hekla, ***which*** *last erupted in 1981.*
Ted Edwards, ***who*** *was once a school drama teacher ...*
First he went to Timbuktu, ***where*** *he bought two camels.*

We use non-defining relative clauses to give extra information about someone or something. We use ***which*** for things or events, ***who*** for people and ***where*** for places.

When writing a non-defining relative clause, we put commas (,) at the beginning of the clause, and at the end if the clause comes in the middle of the sentence.

1

Complete the text about Ted Edwards using *which, who* or *where*.

Ted Edwards, (1) ________ once was a drama teacher, is now an experienced adventurer. In 1983 he set off on a journey across the Sahara Desert, (2) ________ nearly killed him. Certainly the BBC film crew, (3) ________ were waiting for him, did not expect to see him alive.

Next he went to Iceland, (4) ________ he saw spectacular waterfalls, glaciers and volcanoes. He started his journey in Seydisfjordur, (5) ________ is a small town on the East coast. The journey, (6) ________ took him 14 days to complete, took him 510 miles across the island. He finally arrived in Reykjavik, (7) ________ two journalists were waiting for him. They were Barbara and Johann Magnusson, (8) ________ worked for one of the Icelandic daily newspapers.

2

Use *which, who* or *where* to join sentences 1 – 8 with suitable phrases from the box.

1 Ted Edwards is from Lancaster, *where he worked as a drama teacher for ten years.*

2 In 1984 Ted went to Iceland, ________________

3 He climbed Mount Hekla, ________________

4 He also climbed on Vatnajokull, ________________

5 He spent a long time walking across volcanic desert, ________________

6 He met Johann and Barbara Magnusson, ________________

he burnt his leg   are journalists
is an island in the Atlantic Ocean
there are no plants, animals or people
~~he worked as a drama teacher for ten years~~
is the largest glacier in Europe

Language Summary 2

Phrasal verbs

Then he ***set out on*** *his epic journey, but he soon* ***ran into*** *problems.*

Phrasal verbs consist of a verb and a preposition and/or an adverbial particle which usually combine to give a new meaning. Here ***set out on*** = *began* and ***ran into*** = *had.*

3

Match the synonyms in the box with the phrasal verbs in the sentences.

arrived (unexpectedly)   ~~had no more~~   stopped
hope to enjoy   started a journey

1 He got lost and **ran out of water**. *had no more*

2 The BBC television crew ... had **given up** expecting to see him alive. ________

3 I am **looking forward to** showing you my slides. ________

4 They **turned up** to meet me. ________

5 I **set off** on foot across Iceland. ________

Vocabulary

4

Fill in the two missing letters which complete the two words. All the first words are related to entertainment.

1 F E S T I V *A* *L* R E A D Y
2 A C T __ __ G A N I S E
3 T H E A T __ __ S T A U R A N T
4 P R O G R A M __ __ A L
5 C I N E __ __ N A G E R
6 M I __ __ N U
7 M U S I C __ __ W A Y S
8 O P E __ __ N
9 D I S __ __ N C E R T

Language Summary 1

Likes and dislikes

You know people ***enjoy watching*** *good films.*
You ***don't like*** *the idea of a pop group.*

1

Read Suzie's telephone conversation with Brian. Underline the words and phrases expressing opinion.

Suzie: Hi, Brian, it's me, Suzie.

Brian: Oh, hello.

Suzie: I rang to see if you want to come to the cinema tonight.

Brian: The cinema? Well, I don't really like going to the cinema.

Suzie: But it's a season of Francis Ford Coppola films. The Godfather's on tonight ... you know, with Marlon Brando.

Brian: Oh no! I can't stand him. Anyway, I've seen The Godfather – it's really violent.

Suzie: Oh, I love films like that. Anyway, if you're not very keen on the cinema, what about going for a drink?

Brian: Now, that's a better idea. I enjoy going for a drink on a Saturday night.

Suzie: Well, where do you want to go?

Brian: I don't mind. You choose.

Suzie: Well, I'm not very fond of 'Rizzo's Bar' so let's go to 'La Taverna'. I really like their beer.

Now write the words and phrases in the correct column.

Positive	Neutral	Negative
		don't like

Language Summary 2

Expressing agreement and disagreement

I think it's too difficult to get costumes. – ***So do I.***
I don't think this is a good idea. – ***Neither do I.***

We use ***so*** to agree with a positive statement, and ***nor*** or ***neither*** to agree with a negative one. In informal English we can use ***me too*** instead of ***so do I*** or ***me neither*** instead of ***nor do I***.

I don't think the town hall's too small. – ***Well, I do.***

Well /Oh, I do contradicts a negative statement.
Well /Oh, I don't contradicts a positive one.

2

Use the prompts to agree or disagree with these statements.

1 I don't want to see the acrobats. ✘ Oh, I do
2 I think discos are too noisy. ✘ ______
3 I don't like classical concerts. ✔ ______
4 I think fireworks are too expensive. ✔ ______
5 I want to see the late film. ✘ ______
6 I watch TV most nights. ✔ ______
7 I need to buy a ticket. ✔ ______
8 I don't know anything about Tai Chi. ✘ ______

3

Look at these phrases from the lesson. Write A next to the expressions which express agreement and D next to the ones which express disagreement.

1 I don't think ...
2 Now, that's a great idea!
3 OK then.
4 Yeah, that sounds fine.
5 I'm not so sure about that.
6 I think you're right there.

Pronunciation

4

Adjectives and word stress

These adjectives are all from this unit. Write P next to the positive adjectives and N next to the negative adjectives. Then underline the stressed syllables.

amazing	P	entertaining	__	popular	__
awful	__	excellent	__	spectacular	__
boring	__	exciting	__	unusual	__
disappointing	__	interesting	__		

Language Summary 1

Comparatives with *as ... as*

*The Blue Whale can weigh **as** much **as** 150 tonnes.*
*The situation is**n't as** bad **as** that.*

We can use ***as ... as*** with an adjective or adverb to say that two things are the same. We can use ***not as ... as*** to say that two things are NOT the same.

1

Use the table below to make seven comparisons between the lion and the tiger. Use *as ... as* and *not as ... as*.

	lion	tiger
body length	1.7m – 1.9m	1.7m – 1.9m
tail length	90cms	90cms
weight	up to 250kgs	up to 250kgs
maximum jump	8.5 – 9.0m	5.5 – 6.0m
abilities	poor swimmer	good swimmer
cubs (babies)	2–4	2–4
length of time with parents	2–4 years	18 months.

1 *The lion's body is as long as the tiger's.*
2 ____________
3 ____________
4 ____________
5 ____________
6 ____________
7 ____________

Write three more sentences comparing two other animals.

1 ____________
2 ____________
3 ____________

Language Summary 2

Revision of comparatives and superlatives

*The Blue Whale's whistle ... is **louder than** Concorde.*
*It is **the largest** creature that has ever lived.*

(See Unit 2, Lesson 3 and Unit 3, Lesson 1.)

2

Complete the conversation between Helena and Max: Use the comparative or superlative form of the words in brackets and any extra words you need.

Max: What are you reading?

Helena: A wildlife magazine. There's (1) *the most amazing* (amazing) article about bats.

Max: Bats ... ugh! They're (2) ____________ (ugly) animals on Earth!

Helena: Maybe, but they're not (3) ____________ (bad) you think. They're really interesting.

Max: So, what's (4) ____________ (large) bat?

Helena: Well, the one with (5) ____________ (large) wingspan is the 'flying fox'. Its wingspan is 1.5 metres.

Max: That's almost (6) ____________ (wide) a condor's wingspan.

Helena: No, a condor's is (7) ____________ (big). And (8) ____________ (dangerous) bat is a vampire bat because they drink animal blood.

Max: So what's (9) ____________ (interesting) fact you've found out?

Helena: Probably that some bats can fly (10) ____________ (fast) 32 kilometres per hour!

Max: That's (11) ____________ (good) than my car!

Language Summary 3

Revision of the present perfect

*They **have existed** for over 70,000 years.*

(See Unit 4, Lesson 1 and Unit 7, Lesson 1.)

3

Complete the text about sharks using the present perfect form of the verbs in the box.

also/attack ever/attack ~~never/be~~ cause exist
always/hunt ever/live record see

Sharks (1) *have never been* popular creatures since people think they are very dangerous. In fact, out of the 200–250 species of shark that exist, only 27 species (2) ____________ humans. They (3) ____________ small boats. Of all the sharks the white shark (4) ____________ the most problems.

In 1958 a shark research institute was established and since then they (5) ____________ all shark attacks there. One shark that is not dangerous is the whale shark. It is the largest fish that (6) ____________. It usually measures 9 metres in length, but some people say they (7) ____________ whale sharks measuring 18 metres. They can weigh up to 70 tonnes. Sharks (8) ____________ for thousands of years and we (9) ____________ them for food. We also use shark leather to make shoes and belts.

Unit 9 Lesson 2

Language Summary 1

Reported speech

*Police **said** the tenant **was** a civilian.*

When the reporting verb is in the past we usually put the other verb in an earlier time.

eg present simple ***is*** → past simple ***was***
present continuous ***is writing*** → past continuous ***was writing***

*Reinstaedt **told** reporters **that** there **was** a python in the hall.*

We can use ***that*** to join the reported speech to the rest of the sentence –
Police said 'We think he is on holiday.' → Police said (***that***) they thought he was on holiday.

Pronouns in direct speech change in reported speech – eg we → they, I → she/he.

1

Look at police investigator Reinstaedt's comments and write them in reported speech. Use the article on page 56 to help you.

1 The tenant is a civilian.' *Reinstaedt said (that) the tenant was a civilian.*
2 'He is writing a military history book.' ______
3 'We are still looking for him.' ______
4 'The US authorities are helping with enquiries.' ______
5 'He has got over 50 weapons in his flat.' ______
6 'He obviously likes animals too.' ______
7 'There is a crocodile swimming in his bath tub.' ______
8 'He also has a large python in the hall.' ______

Language Summary 2

say* and *tell

*They **said** that they thought he was currently on holiday in the United States.*
*Police **told** reporters that US authorities were helping to locate him.*

We say something (to somebody) – eg *Police **said** …*, but we ***tell*** somebody something – eg *Police **told*** reporters …
We also use ***tell*** in idiomatic expressions – eg ***tell a story/a joke/lies***.

2

Complete the sentences with the correct form of *say* or *tell*.

1 Why didn't you ______ me before?
2 What did the woman ______ to you?
3 Can you ______ that again, please?
4 You mustn't ______ that word again.
5 It's bad to ______ lies.
6 I couldn't understand what she ______
7 He ______ me the news yesterday.
8 The teachers always ______ them a story before school finishes.

Vocabulary

3

Animals

Label the diagrams with words from the box. Use a dictionary to help you.

beak ear fur hoof horn paw feather tail ~~wing~~

Unit 9 Lesson 3

Language Summary 1

Short forms

***Don't** worry, **we're** OK.*
***Having** a great time. (= **I am/We are having** a great time.)*

We usually use contractions in spoken and informal written English – eg in postcards, where we also sometimes miss out obvious words.

1

Write the full forms of these contractions.

1 I've never seen snow before. *I have.*
2 I'd hate to experience a typhoon. ________
3 Well, let's see. It was a few years ago ... ________
4 If it doesn't stop raining it'll be a disaster. ______ ______
5 She's bought a warm coat because they say it'll snow. ________ ________
6 I don't think he'd go sailing in this weather. ________ ________

2

Underline the words in this postcard that could be contracted. Then put brackets ( ) around the words you could miss out.

Hi Constance,

(We are) having a wonderful time here in Italy. We have been to Rome and we have visited the Roman ruins. We are hoping to go to Florence tomorrow. I have got a slight cold at the moment, but do not worry it will soon go, I am sure. Ron has taken lots of photos with his new camera. It is a pity you could not come with us. Anyway, we are looking forward to seeing you.

Love Nicki.

Rewrite the postcard using contractions for the words you have underlined and without the words in brackets.

Language Summary 2

Past continuous

*We **were staying** in a horrible hotel next to the noisiest disco in the town.*

We often use the past continuous to give background descriptions for a story in the past.

*The temperature **was** up in the thirties every day.*
*We **could see** the clouds racing across the skies.*

There are some verbs we do not usually use in the continuous form – eg ***be*** (we use the past tense), and ***see, hear, taste*** and ***believe*** (we sometimes use ***could*** + verb).

3

Read the beginning of this story. Then complete the background description.

Journey of disaster

Dave felt his head and immediately remembered that the plane had crashed. Where was he now? He got to his feet and looked around ...

1 Sun/shine/but/not/hot *The sun was shining but it wasn't hot.*
2 It/dark ________
3 He/not believe/he/alive ________
4 It/rain/very hard ________
5 Strong wind/blow ________
6 He/see/waves crashing/against rocks ________
7 His clothes/very wet and torn ________
8 He/hear/strange noises/but/not see anything ________

Vocabulary

4

Weather

Put the words in the box on the scale below in order of temperature.

boiling ~~cold~~ cool freezing hot warm

cold | ____ | ____ | ____ | ____ | ____ |

Look at the words in the box below. Which of the words are nouns? Which are adjectives? Which are verbs? Write them in the correct column. Note that some can belong to two categories.

cloudy cold drizzle dry foggy hail hot humid rain showers snow sunny sunshine wet wind windy

Adjectives *It will be ...*	**Nouns** *There will be ...*	**Verbs** *It will ...*
cloudy		

Language Summary 1

too **and** *enough*

*The water was **too** fast and dangerous for the dinghies.*
*Dave and Steve didn't think it was safe **enough** to continue.*

We use ***too*** in front of adjectives or adverbs to say that something is in excess.

We use ***enough*** after adjectives and adverbs but in front of nouns to say that something is sufficient.

1

Fill in the gaps with *too* or *enough*, then match the two halves of the sentences.

1 The meat is _too_ tough
2 The sea is ______ dangerous
3 I've got ______ money
4 You aren't studying hard ______
5 I'm ______ ill
6 He's stupid ______

a) to believe you.
b) to eat.
c) to pass the exam.
d) to swim in.
e) to buy a new car.
f) to go to work.

Language Summary 2

Past perfect

*Once the team **had passed** the falls, they put the dinghies back on the river.*

We make the past perfect with ***had*** + **past participle**. We often use it with another clause in the past simple to talk about an event that happened before another event in the past.

— PAST — PAST — PRESENT —

Once the team *had passed* the falls, → they put the dingies back on the water

2

Diana got a place on Blashford Snell's expedition, but she didn't have a very successful trip. Write sentences about what happened using the prompts and the past perfect and past simple.

1 When/reach/airport/flight/already/leave _When she reached the airport, the flight had already left._
2 When/reach/check-in/realize/forget/passport ______
3 Discover/prices/go up/when/buy/another ticket ______
4 Discover/someone/take seat/when/get on/plane ______
5 When/arrive/Addis Ababa/discover/airline/lose/luggage ______
6 When/arrive/expedition headquarters/expedition leave ______

Vocabulary

3

Connectors

Complete the passage using the words and phrases in the box.

At first	but	in the end	The next day	then	while

(1) ______ everything went well but (2) ______ Glen capsized. He survived, (3) ______ the canoe was badly damaged. (4) ______ at the Tississat Falls there was a team crisis: Dave and Steve thought it wasn't safe enough to continue. There was a long argument and (5) ______ the two Mikes continued in their canoes (6) ______ the other three carried their equipment on land.

4

Time expressions

The expedition started on Sunday 8th September. Complete the missing dates.

1 the next Sunday _Sunday 15th September_
2 five days later ______
3 the day before ______
4 the following day ______
5 a fortnight before ______
6 the previous Monday ______
7 a week earlier ______
8 the same day ______

Language Summary 1

have to and _must_ for obligation

*You **have to** calculate exactly how much water you need in the desert.*
*You **must** write a book about your trip.*

We use ***have to* + infinitive** to express obligation, often when it is imposed by something or someone other than the speaker (See Unit 5, Lesson 2).
We can also use ***must*** to express obligation but usually when the speaker thinks something is important.
The past form of both ***have to*** and ***must*** is ***had to***.

*We **didn't have to** worry about wild animals.*
*You **mustn't** get up too late.*

We use **don't *have to* + infinitive** when there is no obligation to do something.

We use ***mustn't*** when there is an obligation NOT to do something.

1

Eric and Lina are in a small town in Chile preparing to cross into Argentina. Eric is waiting for Lina in a café.

Complete their conversation using an appropriate form of *have to* or *must*.

Eric: Hi, Lina, what took you so long?

Lina: Well, I (1) _had to_ buy some extra food and I also (2) __________ go to immigration.

Eric: Oh, right. Well, we certainly (3) __________ worry about food because I've just bought some too.

Lina: I also went to the post office and there was a letter from my brother.

Eric: How is he?

Lina: Well, he (4) __________ go into hospital last Friday for a check-up. Fortunately he (5) __________ have an operation, but I (6) __________ try to ring him when we reach the next place with a phone.

Eric: Well, I've been looking at the map and we (7) __________ set off early tomorrow morning. We (8) __________ try to reach the border when it opens.

Lina: But, we (9) __________ forget to collect the passports first – I (10) __________ leave them at immigration this afternoon.

Eric: Oh no. And we (11) __________ repair the tent before we go or we'll get very wet tomorrow night. And I (12) __________ leave the bikes unlocked tonight – someone might steal them.

Language Summary 2

Revision of the *-ing* form

*We cycled past glaciers and saw them **crashing** into lakes.*
(See Unit 7, Lesson 3).

2

Complete the sentences using the words in the box.

barking blowing burning ~~crashing~~ darkening falling jumping shouting

1 We saw glaciers _crashing_ into the lakes.
2 We stood by the lake and saw fish __________ up out of the water.
3 As we crossed the desert we could feel the sun __________ our skin.
4 It was difficult to cycle with the wind __________ against us.
5 We looked out of the tent to see the sky __________
6 Half an hour later we woke up to the sound of rain __________ onto the tent.
7 One night we were frightened when we heard people ____ for help.
8 Then we couldn't get back to sleep because of the dogs __________ on the farm.

Vocabulary

3

Collocations

Which of the nouns in the box can go with these adjectives? Some of the nouns go with more than one adjective.

desert forest mountains rain rivers ~~sea~~ sky snow trees water wind

deep _sea,_ __________
dry __________
heavy __________
high __________
icy __________
strong __________
tall __________
thick __________

Unit 10 Lesson 3

Language Summary 1

Revision of future forms

Present continuous

Our unit ***is sending*** *a four-month expedition to Antarctica next spring.*

We can use the present continuous for future arrangements. (See Unit 1 Lesson 3.)

going to

We are a team of six scientists who ***are going to*** *visit Libya some time next year.*

We also use ***going to*** for future arrangements and intentions.
(See Unit 3, Lesson 3.)

will

Unfortunately the expedition ***will*** *be expensive.*

We can use ***will*** for predictions. (See Unit 4, Lesson 3.)

1

Complete the conversation between Han and his friend, George, using a future form of the verbs in brackets.

George: Where (1) are you going (you/go) on your expedition?

Han: We (2) __________ (go) to the Amazon jungle. In fact we (3) __________ (fly) to Rio on Monday so we (4)__________ (probably/do) some sightseeing before flying to Manaus on Thursday.

George: What do you think the climate (5) __________ (be) like?

Han: Well, they say that it (6) __________ (be) very hot, but dry. It (7) __________(not/rain) but I'm sure it (8) __________(be) humid. Anyway, we (9) __________ (take) lots of sun cream and our waterproofs.

George: Who else (10) __________ (go)?

Han: Julia is, but it's an international project so 30 people from different countries (11) __________(go).

George: It sounds great. I'm sure you (12) __________ (have) fun.

Language Summary 2

hope to* and *hope (that)

We ***hope to*** *go to India next year.*
We ***hope (that)*** *you will be able to support us.*

We use ***hope to*** or ***hope that*** to talk about something we want to happen.

When the subjects of ***hope*** and the second verb are the same we use ***hope to***.

When the subjects are different we use ***hope (that)***.

2

Alick is talking about the plans for his expedition. Write sentences using the prompts, *hope to* or *hope that*, and a suitable verb.

1 We/Vietnam. We hope to go to Vietnam.
2 We/three months __________
3 I/not rain/too much __________
4 We/Snow Leopard __________
5 We/plant studies __________
6 I/expedition/not/too expensive __________
7 We/sponsorship __________
8 I/we/good photographs __________
9 I/no problems __________

Writing

3

Formal letters

The numbers on this letter refer to eight different parts of the letter. Write the correct number next to the name of each part.

a writer's signature 7
b ending the letter ___
c writer's address ___
d greeting ___
e the date ___
f receiver's name ___
g writer's name ___
h receiver's address ___

The Adventure Foundation Trust

[1] The Adventure Foundation Trust
Enfield Street
LONDON W3

[2] 23 March 1995

Ms Maria Hamilton [3]
Hillbury High School[4]
Dover
Kent

Dear Ms Hamilton, [5]

Thank you for your letter of March 17th.

We were very interested to hear about your proposed expedition to Iceland, but unfortunately we are unable to sponsor you.

We wish you good luck with your plans.

Yours sincerely, [6]

Brenda McSharry [7]

Brenda McSharry [8]